SACRED
ENCOUNTERS
with Jesus

SACRED
ENCOUNTERS
with Jesus

G. Scott Sparrow, Ed.D.

ThomasMore®

from Ave Maria Press, Inc. • Notre Dame, IN

NIHIL OBSTAT:
Rev. Msgr. Glenn D. Gardner, J.C.D.
Censor Librorum

IMPRIMATUR:
† Most Rev. Charles V. Grahmann
Bishop of Dallas

September 16, 2002

The Nihil Obstat and Imprimatur are official declarations that the material
reviewed is free of doctrinal or moral error. No implication is contained therein that
those granting the Nihil Obstat and Imprimatur agree with the contents, opinions,
or statements expressed.

Acknowledgment
The Scripture quotations contained herein are from the *New Revised Standard Version
Bible: Catholic Edition* copyright © 1993 and 1989 by the Division of Christian
Education for the National Council of the Churches of Christ in the U.S.A. Used by
permission. All rights reserved.

Send all inquiries to:
Thomas More® Publishing
P.O. Box 428
Notre Dame, IN 46556
Visit us at: www.avemariapress.com

Printed in the United States of America

Library of Congress Control Number: 2002109874

ISBN 0-88347-498-0

For Ryan

Contents

Foreword

IT IS ASTOUNDING ENOUGH THAT JESUS APPEARED to his disciples and friends after his death. It is even more astounding that he has never ceased appearing. Indeed, from the accounts presented in this book, we can reasonably conclude that Jesus still appears today—healing and transforming people just as he ministered to his brokenhearted and defeated disciples. Once the despairing band of ordinary men and women experienced the risen Jesus, they went forth exhibiting an incredible faith and love that eventually conquered the mighty Roman Empire that had tried to destroy them. Similarly, when people experience Christ today, they find encouragement, help in the midst of darkness, and sometimes healing of the mind and body. Further, Christ instills the conviction that, ultimately, all will be well—and that the eternal love they have experienced in this world will be theirs in the world to come.

Sacred Encounters with Jesus is a discerning and comprehensive account of how people still experience Christ today. What is surprising to me is that no one has previously taken the trouble to collect and explain the meaning of these experiences. This fascinating book conveys a wealth of both religious and psychological wisdom.

There has been a recent interest in angels and their appearances to individuals. In response to this growing interest, major news publications have been more willing to report experiences of these more-than-human realities with which humans can nonetheless relate and communicate. Within the Christian tradition, however, the risen Christ is closer to the Divine than even the angelic hosts. If so, then the experiences of Christ related in *Sacred Encounters with Jesus* will likely bring readers even closer to the eternal reality that we can know in this life, and convey a deeper understanding of the nature of everlasting life.

For over forty years, I have been studying the religious experiences that form the foundation of all the great religions.[1] However, much of Western religion has been influenced and contaminated by an overly materialistic worldview. This view suggests that *only* the physical world is real and human beings are limited to the information that they receive through the five physical senses.

John Polkinghorne, physicist, theologian, and president of Queen's College, Cambridge, reminds us that *both* theology and theoretical physics deal with a world that cannot be experienced directly through the five senses. From this viewpoint, the spiritual world is just as real as the physical one.

But why is contact with the spiritual world so apparently rare? Several thinkers have suggested that our physical experiences are filtered through the reducing valve of the brain and nervous system. The information that comes out of this reducing valve concerns only that data which is necessary to keep us alive in this physical world.

In my years of study into religious experiences, I have found that the dream is the natural altered state of consciousness through which all of us make nightly contact with that realm of reality that has not been filtered through the reducing valve of the brain and senses. Visions differ from dreams *only because we experience them while we are awake* rather than asleep. Although the content of the dream is the same as that of a vision, in visions we are in touch with two different realms of reality at the same time. Hallucinations can occur whenever we lose the ability to tell the difference between the vision and our waking world.

In meditation, another fertile arena for receiving visionary experiences, we can enter the realm of the dream and vision, and can even encounter the Creator. Sometimes when this happens, the Holy One appears as ineffable light, and sometimes as the risen Jesus. In other experiences, individuals may perceive an angel, another religious figure, or a formless sense of divine presence. Because of the vast scope of these experiences, the author has quite wisely limited himself to experiences of the risen or eternal Christ.

Jesus began appearing to people immediately after his death. After he was crucified by the Romans on the day before Passover in A.D. 29, his terrified disciples hid, fearing that they might be sought out and meet their Master's fate. On Sunday Jesus appeared first of all to Mary Magdalene, whose grief turned into pure joy; he next fell into step on the road to Emmaus with two grieving followers and revealed himself to them as he broke the bread they prepared to eat together. Then he vanished. These two awestruck followers of Jesus ran back to Jerusalem to share their incredible good news with the hiding disciples. Then they all saw Jesus standing in their midst in his glorified, transcendent body, and he disappeared again. Jesus' numerous appearances prepared his friends, family members, and disciples to expect him to make good on his promise to always be present with them.

Twice more Jesus appeared: first to Thomas, and later to the disciples fishing on the Sea of Galilee. Then came a final parting when Jesus disappeared from their sight in a blaze of glory. This event is particularly significant. They knew that they would not experience him in the same physical-spiritual body again, but they had come to understand that he was still just as much present as when they walked the roads of Galilee together. They knew that he would always be with them, and that they had lost nothing. Instead of sorrow, they returned to Jerusalem with great joy to await the gift of the Holy Spirit. Had modern physicists or astronomers been present, they might have used the words of Howard Chandler Robbins' hymn to describe their experience.

> *And have the bright immensities received our risen Lord,*
> *Where light-years frame the Pleiedes and point Orion's sword?*
> *Do flaming suns his footsteps trace through corridors sublime,*
> *The Lord of interstellar space and Conqueror of time?*
>
> *The heaven that hides him from our sight knows neither*
> *near nor far;*
> *An altar candle sheds its light as surely as a star,*
> *And where his loving people meet to share the gift divine;*
> *There stands he with unhurrying feet, there heavenly*
> *splendors shine.*[2]

For nearly two thousand years people have continued to experience the presence of the risen, cosmic Christ. Some momentous events of world history have occurred because of encounters with this Being. Saul of Tarsus encountered Christ as an orb of blinding light on the road to Damascus. As he was going there to persecute Jesus' followers in that city, he heard the words of Christ, "I am Jesus whom thou persecutest," and was transformed. Then Christ appeared to Ananias. Against his will, Ananias met with Saul and helped make him into a new man—Paul the Apostle to the Greek world.

For nearly three centuries, Christians were persecuted throughout the Roman Empire. Then the emperor Constantine had a vision of a flaming cross in the sky and heard the words: "In this sign you will conquer."

The emperor could make no sense of the sign until Jesus appeared to him in a dream carrying the symbol and explained that it was made of the first two letters of Christ in Greek. Under this sign Constantine defeated the pagan emperors who had been persecuting Christians for nearly three hundred years. One of Constantine's first acts was to abolish the persecution of Christians. It is difficult for us to imagine the momentous impact of his decision upon the Christian fellowship and upon world history.

Hundreds of years later, Saint Francis of Assisi was praying before a crucifix and had a vision of Jesus speaking to him. With this inspiration Francis became a model of divine love and revived a dormant and cynical church. Jesus had come again at a crucial moment in the unfoldment of his church.

John Newton was the captain of a slave ship until he dreamed of meeting the Christ who saved him from disaster. He left his infamous trading, went to seminary, and became a minister. He wrote many of the greatest Christian hymns, among them "Amazing Grace." His dream of a forgiving Christ was the amazing grace that saved him.

A few years later, in 1895, one of the leading pastors in the Baptist Church, A. J. Gordon, wrote his spiritual autobiography. In it he described a powerful dream in which he noticed a stranger in the church, but he forgot to look for him after the service. He asked a man who had sat next to the stranger who the stranger was. The gentleman replied: "Why, do you not know that man? It was Jesus of Nazareth." Gordon expressed his dismay at not meeting Jesus. The man replied nonchalantly: "Oh, do not be troubled. He has been here today, and no doubt he will come again." Gordon never preached another sermon without remembering Jesus' words, "Lo, I am with you always." It was the turning point of his ministry.[3]

In his book *Beyond the Mirror*, Henri Nouwen, a Catholic priest and a widely read writer, has provided a superb description of an experience of the cosmic and personal Christ. At a time when his life hung in the balance, he entered the portals of death and found the risen Jesus there with arms open to embrace him. He also realized that this figure was there for him, personally, and at the same time was embracing the whole universe.

This experience was cleansing, healing, and powerful. As he reflected on this experience of Christ's love, Nouwen realized he needed new theological language to convey the depth and breadth of Jesus' all-encompassing caring.[4]

Transforming religious experiences are far more common than we ordinarily realize. In a careful sociological survey, Andrew Greeley discovered that 39 percent of the people surveyed said "yes" to this question: "Have you ever felt as though you were very close to a powerful, spiritual force that seemed to lift you out of yourself?" Greeley discovered that fully half of these people had never told another human being of their experience because they were afraid they would be ridiculed. He also found that religious professionals were the last people with whom this group of people would share their religious experiences.[5]

At an ecumenical conference of some two hundred people, I invited the attendees to write down their most important religious experiences and share them with me. Fully half of the fifty accounts I received described the appearance of Christ—indeed, this was the most significant part of their experience. Thus, these experiences described by Dr. Sparrow need to be taken very seriously, for the healing, loving Christ is nearer than we usually realize.

This truth became evident to me some time ago. During a time of inner turmoil and conflict, I learned to listen to my dreams. With the help of a Jewish Jungian analyst, who had escaped from a Nazi concentration camp, I began to see that my dreams were trying to show me the way out off the dead-end street on which I found myself. As I learned the language of dreams and realized I was being led by the Spirit, it then occurred to me that if the Holy One was trying to lead me in my sleep, then this same reality would be available if I consciously turned toward the risen Christ in utter quiet and utter honesty. Eventually, I found that whenever I was in real need and was unable to help myself, I could call out and a light would appear. Out of the light, the cosmic and yet intensely personal Jesus would appear and lead me out of crisis.

One of my most helpful dreams came at a time of real doubt. A part of me doubted that I had a real message to share at the seminary where I was speaking. That night I dreamed of an intense but healing light. In the dream I fell on my knees in awe and wonder. I knew I was in the presence of the Divine.

The light gradually took the form of a human being who walked toward me. I was fearful, but this person took me by the hand, raised me to my feet, and embraced me. I knew it was Christ, but I was afraid to ask his name. When I did he laughingly said: "Hardly Visible." We talked for a while and then he disappeared. I wrote down the dream, went back to sleep, and by morning the darkness and doubt had disappeared and I was able to share the victory and eternal presence of the risen Christ with those who were waiting for me to speak.[6]

—Morton Kelsey

Introduction

WHEN I FIRST BEGAN RESEARCHING SACRED encounters with Jesus, I was doing psychotherapy with a young man who was struggling with a long-term addiction. I knew that his devotion to Christ was the one thing that kept him from giving up entirely, so we often talked about Jesus' love for and acceptance of his unruly disciples, in spite of their flaws.

One day when he was feeling particularly despondent, we were talking about people who had experienced Christ's direct intervention in their lives—including Bill Wilson, the founder of AA. My client expressed a hope that Jesus would intervene in his life, too, since his own efforts had failed. As he talked on about his deep desire for such an intervention, I found myself praying that his yearning would be fulfilled.

Suddenly, I was "struck" by what felt like a wave of energy coming from my left. I knew from my own encounters with Jesus that this feeling often precedes his coming. I continued to sit in silence, looking at and listening to my client as usual, not knowing where this was going. After a few moments, my client stopped talking in mid-sentence, looked in the direction from which I had felt the wave of energy come, and then said, "What's happening? Something's happening here." Then a second, stronger wave hit and I felt almost overwhelmed by it—like I was becoming a child again, and overshadowed by someone with tremendous power and love. I suggested that we close our eyes and be still. As we did, I saw white light. The sense of radiance and love lasted for several minutes. Later on when we talked about the incident, we discovered that we had both felt a palpable sense of Christ's presence with us. Although neither of us actually saw him, we had no doubt that our prayers had been answered.

In the ensuing chapters, I present a variety of similarly remarkable experiences in which individuals believe that Christ came to them in waking visions or deep, unforgettable dreams. Taken together, these experiences raise the possibility that some people will readily accept and others will summarily dismiss—that Jesus can be experienced as directly and as personally today as when he walked the earth two thousand years ago.

The reader will enter into the miraculous experience of a terminally ill little girl who was healed by Jesus' touch after her parents had already said their final good-byes; share the shock of a psychotherapist who turned to see Jesus walking beside her one day; and feel the incredulous wonder of a woman who reached up and touched Jesus' hair as he knelt beside her and prayed. The reader will feel the shame of the young woman who railed at the unavailability of God, only to turn and see Christ smiling warmly at her unbelief; sense the anxiety of a young man who faced a stern but loving Jesus intent on showing him the mess he'd made; and feel the relief of a dejected woman who heard Christ say to her, "You always have *me*."

These accounts convey a simple message: that we can know Jesus as personally as those who followed him during his walk among us.

Given the sensitive and controversial nature of these experiences, I believe the reader should know that I bring to this project something in addition to a researcher's point of view: I bring the memories of my own encounter experiences with Christ.

My first of several such experiences, most of which have been lucid dreams,[7] took place in 1975. I dreamed that I was actually flying around inside a new building with my friend Mark. It seemed we were involved in praying for, or consecrating, the building. At one point, I saw Mark standing in a doorway at the back of the auditorium, talking to someone beyond the threshold. I knew it was Jesus! Knowing then that I was dreaming, I eagerly walked toward the door, hoping he would still be there. I passed through the door and looked toward where I assumed he would be. At first I was only able to see bright white light. But then I could see a man clearly in the midst of the light. He was strikingly handsome.

I stood silent and awed by his presence. I felt great love from him, but a sternness as well. He finally asked me, *"Are you ready to leave the earth yet?"* I realized that he was asking if I was ready to die. Startled by the implications of his question, I said, "No." He then said, *"Then go out and do what you know to do."*

Looking back, I realize that I was wavering at that time in my commitment to the path of service I had chosen. It should come as little surprise that the dream effectively nudged me back on course. His words still remind me to take stock of the work I am doing, and whether it serves him.

Like many of the individuals whose experiences are recounted in the following chapters, I didn't have a conscious personal relationship with Jesus Christ prior to the onset of these experiences. My rather liberal Christian upbringing somehow allowed me to circumvent the whole awkward issue of a personal and ongoing relationship with Christ.

Even after undertaking a daily practice of Christ-centered meditation and prayer during my freshman year in college—which I have continued ever since—the person Jesus did not seem, at that time, very important to me. But once the experiences with Jesus started to happen, I began to awaken to the fact that he had been, and would continue to be, the central person in my life.

Not long ago, my son Ryan told me about an experience he had had the night before. He remembers crawling out of bed and heading down the hallway toward our room to get in bed with us, as was customary at the time. Before he reached our door, however, he saw "this light" reach all the way up to the ceiling. Then he saw a man in the light, a man with a beard whom he knew was Jesus. I asked him how he felt when he saw Jesus. Ryan said, "I was afraid!" When I asked him what else happened, he said that Jesus told him not to be afraid. Then Jesus "vanished" and Ryan awakened in his bed, and realized that he had been dreaming.

Why did Ryan dream of Jesus? Perhaps it was because we had read to him about Jesus and the disciples from the time he was an infant. Maybe it was because he eagerly goes to Sunday school every week. Or perhaps it was because I had told him months before something that most of us never consider. I had suggested that he *could* dream of Jesus. And regardless of what one believes about such experiences, one thing is certain: Ryan has come to think of Jesus as someone he can *know*.

I sincerely hope that this book will help many people come to think of Jesus that way, and that it will be seen as a step in the right direction toward providing a forum for sharing experiences that heretofore—for various reasons—have been kept as personal treasures from the world at large.

1

The Christ Encounter Phenomenon

I heard the voice of my Jesus say,
"Come unto me and rest."
Edgar Cayce

LAURA'S DOCTORS WERE SURE THAT SHE WAS DYING. Laura, her mother, and her sister had all contracted scarlet fever, but her illness had progressed into spinal meningitis, for which there was no medical treatment at the time. The doctors told her parents they could do nothing, and that she would die a horrible death. Her parents were advised not to remain with her to witness her last days. Here is Laura's account in her own words:

I am now a grandmother, age sixty-two. For many years I never spoke of my Christ experience. I wish now that I had looked up the records so today I could have the proof nonbelievers seem to need. Somewhere I know there is some proof in hospital and church records, as I was called the "Miracle Child."

Today I can't remember the dates. I was eleven years old, living in Ohio. My mother, sister, and I had scarlet fever—my own went into spinal meningitis.

My parents had lost everything. My father, a carpenter by trade, had been unemployed for a long time. The state of Ohio paid my hospital bills and even flew in a doctor from Chicago. The part of Ohio State University Hospital that I was in was a building apart from the main hospital with a high fence around it. I don't remember going in, but I remember my father carrying me out.

I remember one of the nine times that I was held in a tight ball and told not to move, as they injected a big needle in my spine. Later, looking in a mirror, for years I could see and count those nine marks. I remember the horrible pain and my thin, twisted legs.

My parents were told my death would be a terrible thing; that it would be best for them not to see or hear, to go home. I lost my sight and hearing, but before that, I saw my parents, grandparents, and the Reverend John Lang standing in the door of my room, not permitted to come in. The smiles, the thrown kisses, the waving good-bye I remember, and then the sea of pain.

Later, after losing my eyesight, I was lying on my right side. I heard a voice behind me say, "Laura, turn over." I said, "No, it hurts too much to move. You come around to this side of the bed." Then the voice said, "I promise you it will not *hurt—turn over." Turning, I saw Jesus. I remember no other words Jesus said to me, yet I know we talked. I watched his beautifully shaped hand reach out and touch my leg.*

Sometime later, I remember remarking to a nurse about what pretty red hair she had. She looked at me in shocked surprise and rushed from the room. The room soon filled up with doctors asking questions. I was a very shy person and there were too many doctors, too many questions. I had to talk about this to the Reverend Lang. He was the one person in all the world I wasn't too shy to talk to.

The Reverend Lang listened, asked questions, and took many notes. I couldn't see the face of Christ, as it was like looking into a light bulb. But his clothes, the color and material I had never seen—all that I can remember. I was very blonde with very pale skin—the skin of Christ was much darker. The color of a piece of his hair I saw fall on his left shoulder as he reached out his left hand to touch me was a color I had never seen. The Reverend Lang called it auburn.

My parents were told I could not live—I did. I sat in a chair and heard I would never walk—I did. They were told I would never have children—I had three.

I had not seen the Reverend Lang for years when I saw in a local paper that he was to speak at a church nearby. My sister and I were late so we slipped in a side door. The Reverend Lang was speaking about a little girl, a "miracle child" he had known, who had seen and was healed by Christ. Here he was telling hundreds of people of the thing that had happened to me—the things we had talked about long ago. He also said the child had a light about her for days after the visit—something I had not known.

This visit from Christ was never spoken of in my home by my family. I was raised thinking it was something you did not talk about. (L.B.K.)

Laura's experience was an intensely private encounter in the confines of her own blinded state of approaching death. But to the extent that it can still inspire us with the transformative love that she experienced in that moment of healing years ago, it is relevant to us today. Indeed, her account serves to demonstrate how one person's apparent encounter with Christ can continue to inspire hope, if not actual healing, in others who hear or read about it.

Was Laura's experience what it seemed to be? That is, did Christ actually heal her? And, more importantly for the rest of us, does Christ really manifest himself to individuals today? This might seem like a naive and childish wish to some. But if we take seriously the promises Christ made to manifest himself to those who love him and serve him, it requires little stretch of the imagination to answer, Why not? And if we add to this the modern-day testimony of a widening circle of credible witnesses, then we might conclude—with some wonder—Yes, he does.

A Largely Overlooked Phenomenon

Contemporary Christ encounters have thus far received scant attention from theologians and ministers—those who might be expected to recognize their significance. T.R. Morton, author of

---

Each account is identified by the person's initials. Most of the accounts have only the person's initials, which indicates that there is only one person with those initials, and they have only one account in the book. If more than one person has the same initials, a number has been placed before the initials to set each person apart. For example, "1st R.P." signifies the second account of a person whose initials are the same as at least one other person.

Knowing Jesus, points to the obvious reason the church and its spokesmen have tended to overlook and discredit such accounts.

We can well appreciate how the church has always been a bit suspicious of an individual's claim to know Jesus by himself. When you acknowledge the claim, you open the door to all kinds of strange, subjective ideas. You give individual experience precedence over the wisdom of the past. Personal knowledge is always a challenge to accepted opinions and a threat to established institutions. . . . It is no wonder that the church has been chary of these claims.

This attitude is by no means a recent development. Actually, the church's position developed in the second century, when a man by the name of Montanus claimed to be receiving messages from the risen Christ. Montanus maintained that Christ would soon be returning to erect the New Jerusalem in Montanus's home province in Asia Minor. The church authorities saw this as a self-serving prophecy that would establish a dangerous precedent, and declared it a heresy.[8]

Montanus claimed that Christ was speaking *through* him. This conferred upon him an authority that no ordinary person could hope to dispute. But what I've found in my research is that most Christ encounters have Christ speaking *to the individual about his love for them.* Such interventions seem to inspire spiritual work without bestowing political or moral advantage upon the recipient.

Some Christ encounters of this type can be found in the writings of a few contemporary figures who are somewhat outside of mainstream Christianity. For example, Starr Daily, the author of *Love Can Open Prison Doors* and many other books on the Christian life, says that his life as a hardened criminal abruptly ended when Jesus came to him in a dream. After a tortuous stint in prison, Daily said he saw "the man whom I'd been trying to hate for years, Jesus the Christ." In the dream, Daily encountered Jesus in a garden. Jesus came toward him:

> . . . *his lips moving as though in prayer. He stopped near me eventually and stood looking down. I had never seen such love in human eye; I had never felt so utterly enveloped in love. I seemed to know consciously that I had seen and felt something that would influence my life throughout all eternity.*[9]

It is interesting that Daily had often dreamed as a child of meeting Jesus in the same garden environment, but had gradually forgotten the dreams. Significantly, Daily follows a largely forgotten age-old Christian tradition in regarding the dream as an acceptable avenue for directly encountering the Christ. Daily went on from this experience to author numerous books on the healing power of faith in Christ.

Edgar Cayce is a controversial figure who reportedly experienced several encounters with Christ during his lifetime. Known principally for his clairvoyant gift that permitted him, while in trance, to give people readings on the treatment of their diseases, he was a deeply religious Christian and an immensely popular Presbyterian Sunday school teacher. And yet he never made his Christ encounters a matter of public record. One of the only ways that we know about his experiences is through a letter he wrote to a friend in 1939:

> . . . *often I have felt, seen, and heard the Master at hand. Just a few days ago I had an experience which I have*

not even told the folk here. As you say, they are too scary to tell, and we wonder at ourselves when we attempt to put them into words, whether we are to believe our own ears, or if others feel we are exaggerating or drawing on our imagination; but to us indeed they are often that which we feel if we hadn't experienced we could not have gone on.

This past week I have been quite "out of the running," but Wednesday afternoon when going into my little office or den for the 4:45 meditation, as I knelt by my couch I had the following experience: First a light gradually filled the room with a golden glow that seemed to be very exhilarating, putting me in a buoyant state. I felt as if I were being given a healing. Then as I was about to give the credit to members of our own group who meet at this hour for meditation (as I felt each and every one of them were praying for and with me), he came. He stood before me for a few minutes in all the glory that he must have appeared to the three on the Mount. Like yourself, I heard the voice of my Jesus say, "Come unto me and rest."[10]

Psychiatrist George Ritchie has reported one of the most detailed Christ encounters in his book, *Return from Tomorrow.*[11] While his Christ encounter has been thought of as primarily a near-death experience—perhaps the most famous NDE on record, since it inspired Raymond Moody to begin his research for his best-selling book *Life After Life*[12] —it is still, above all, an encounter with Jesus Christ. As we shall see in the following chapters, very little meaningful distinction can be made between near-death Christ encounters and those occurring in nonlife-threatening circumstances.

While Ritchie was ill with pneumonia, he was administered a drug to which he reacted so severely that he was considered clinically dead for several minutes prior to his resuscitation. During this interval, he experienced an encounter with Jesus, and an escorted view of the afterlife.

As in so many Christ encounters, when Christ appeared to Ritchie he realized that:

This person was power itself, older than time and yet more modern than anyone I'd ever met.

Above all, with that same mysterious inner certainty, I knew that this man loved me. Far more even than power, what emanated from this Presence was unconditional love. An astonishing love. A love beyond my wildest imagining. This love knew every unlovable thing about me . . . and accepted and loved me just the same.[13]

One might think that such experiences would come to a very few devout individuals. But I have discovered in my preliminary research that Christ encounters apparently happen as much to ordinary individuals who are simply striving in their own way to do their best. From a scriptural standpoint, this is what we might expect, for Jesus made it clear to his followers that he would manifest himself to anyone who loved him and followed his commandments:

They who have my commandments and keep them are those who love me; and those who love me will be loved by my Father, and I will love them and reveal myself to them (John 14:21).

Understandably, most of us give this promise little thought. Or if we do, we disqualify ourselves without examining the reasons.

Feeling unworthy, we may assume that Christ would manifest only to those who live exceedingly virtuous lives; and this rules most of us out. Or, feeling insignificant in the cosmic scheme of things, we assume that he would manifest himself only to individuals who have far greater needs than our own. In this vein, a former patient of mine, who prayerfully called upon the assistance of spirit guides, told me that Jesus had much more important things to do than to attend to her.

Even if we allowed ourselves to hope for such a visitation on the basis of Jesus' recorded promises, what if he did not come? Would that not underscore our sense of unworthiness? Or, maybe worse yet, if he did come, what would he require of us? A nurse dreamed she looked out the window and saw the bright light of the rising sun and Jesus knocking on the emergency room door. Not wanting to face him, she went up to the window and closed the blinds. I can still see the anguish in her face as she told me about this—her one and only Christ encounter. Another person intentionally sought an encounter with Christ, and thereafter dreamed that a basement door opened in her home, and light poured out. She knew Christ was coming up the steps and would appear at any moment. She ran to the door and slammed it shut.

How many of us are ready for such a meeting? Are we willing to expose ourselves to someone who is "power itself," and who knows and loves us completely?

Evaluating the Validity of Christ Encounters

As you read the Christ encounters in the following chapters, you may be inspired by many, unmoved by some, and even offended by a few. We are all different, and we respond to such accounts based on our own beliefs and past experiences. Given our differences in sentiment and worldview, how can we establish the validity of such deeply personal and controversial spiritual experiences? How can we know if they are what they purport to be?

There are precedents that can assist us in this regard. Evaluating the validity of spiritual experiences, especially prophetic pronouncements, is an age-old concern. In the Old Testament, Jeremiah suggested a simple test of validity—that the prophecy come to pass! He said that "when the word of that prophet comes true, then it will be known that the LORD has truly sent the prophet (Jeremiah 28:9)." Building on this proposition, Jesus said, "By the fruits, ye shall know them." This rule effectively broadens Jeremiah's criterion of factual accuracy into one that we might call "goodness of outcome," and is clearly more applicable to experiences that do not contain prophetic information, but nonetheless claim to be of God.

By making the *goodness* that we do the sole criterion by which we are judged, Jesus implies that we should not become overly concerned with the differences between peoples' beliefs and experiences. Unfortunately, a person's beliefs, and the particular details of their personal spiritual experiences, have traditionally figured much more prominently than the fruits of their lives in determining their treatment from others. Indeed, concern about the validity of spiritual beliefs and experiences reached extreme proportions during the days of the Inquisition, when even many of the most devout individuals came under suspicion.

The plight of Saint Teresa of Avila is a good example of how attempts to evaluate spiritual experiences have too often mirrored the fears and biases of the evaluators. The young and vivacious Carmelite nun began seeing Jesus appear to her on a regular basis, sometimes when she would be conversing with the visitors who came to the monastery each day. When the local church authorities, who were threatened by her growing influence, found out about her visions, they called for an investigation which immediately threatened her life. Everyone knew she would be burned if her experiences were judged demonic by the Inquisition. Fortunately, a sympathetic Jesuit intervened to supervise the investigation, and to protect her from the harshest remedies of the Inquisition.

But while her Jesuit protector was temporarily away, Teresa was forced by less sympathetic church officials to do something totally repugnant to her: She was told to test the vision by making an obscene gesture to the Lord. "If it is the devil," the inquisitor argued, "he may take it as an expression of your contempt, and if it is the Lord, he will not hold it against you, for you are merely obeying an order which I have given you to protect our holy faith."

With great sadness, she complied. "This business . . ." she related, "caused me the greatest sorrow, for my next vision was one of the suffering Lord." Even so, Christ knew her heart, and he did not abandon her for her compliance.[14]

Eventually, even the considerable authority of the Inquisition could not discredit Teresa. One of the most unyielding inquisitors finally acknowledged the authenticity of her visions. She went on to reestablish the Carmelite order as a beacon of spirituality during a relatively corrupt and materialistic era.

Given the presumption involved in trying to validate a Christ encounter, I have made little attempt to conduct this evaluation for the reader, except to apply Jesus' own criterion—that is, to examine the "fruits" in the person's life.

The Problem of Telling Other People

Samuel Johnson once said, "Wonders are willingly told and willingly heard." And yet it seems apparent that the act of sharing a religious experience is strewn with interpersonal difficulties. When someone believes he has encountered Jesus Christ, an intimidating set of problems arises to legislate against sharing this otherwise wondrous experience with others.

Some may be afraid that their experience will be seen as corny and all-too-conventional. Others probably worry about being seen as inflated with their own sense of importance. And still others may refrain from disclosing the details of such encounters because they are afraid of being judged crazy, or called liars of the worst kind. In many of the letters I've received from persons who believe they have encountered Christ, the letters begin with such words as, "I know you won't believe me, but. . . ."

There is also the problem of stirring up feelings of inadequacy in other people who have not had such experiences. Even if they share a worldview, which allows for such encounters, it is by no means a sure thing that they will be secure enough in their own spirituality to hear it with an open mind. Jesus admonished his followers to "tell no man" about what they'd experienced with him; and his statement about not casting one's pearls before swine puts the warning in harsher terms.

Even religious authorities may not be able to hear about Christ encounters with an open mind. One woman told us that she finally worked up her nerve to share her Jesus experience with two different priests. The first man listened to what she told him, then resumed talking about altogether unrelated matters, as though he had not even heard her. The second priest became angry, saying that he had sought such an experience all his life. Who was she, he asked, to have been so blessed by Jesus' presence? In recognition of this dilemma, C.S. Lewis wrote: "Once the layman was anxious to hide the fact that he believed so much less than the vicar; he now tends to hide the fact that he believes so much more."[15]

It is not surprising that people generally refrain from sharing such experiences. Unfortunately, their silence creates the impression that Christ encounters are less common than they actually are. This book provides a vehicle for sharing these experiences without fear of the sticky interpersonal problems cited. By preserving the anonymity of contributors, they can relate their Christ encounters without having to worry about reactions from others.

On the receiving end, the sympathetic reader is perhaps in a much better position to appreciate the experiences without knowing the contributors, or having them present. By reading multiple accounts of anonymous, ordinary individuals, the reader might more easily resist the inclination to conclude that the other person is a better, more virtuous individual who deserves to have such encounters. And, relieved of the burden of knowing the other person's foibles, the reader may also be able to appreciate the validity of the account without letting his knowledge of the other person get in the way. Thus, except for losing whatever benefits might proceed from a direct person-to-person exchange, a collection of anonymous written accounts can, arguably, assist both witnesses and readers in reaping the greatest benefit from Christ encounters.

The Positive Impact of Sharing Christ Encounters

Not all Christ encounters are equally dramatic and uplifting. Some are subtle and open-ended, and it is not always clear exactly what has taken place. And yet they almost always seem to represent a pivotal moment in a person's life, in which encouragement or healing seems desperately needed, or in which Christ calls the individual to serve him in some way.

Many of us would be disappointed if we set about to experience a Christ encounter. For reasons unknown to us at the present time, such experiences are still apparently hard to come by. Consequently, we should perhaps be willing to derive whatever meaning we can from the experiences of others, rather than to make such experiences a criterion of spiritual attainment, or the basis of our self-worth. There is ample precedent for this approach. The history of Christianity reveals a willingness among Christians to study and derive sustenance from the experiences of others, rather than feeling disenfranchised in the face of the apparent good fortune of others. The whole historic foundation of Christianity is based on Jesus' encounters with a relatively small group of followers and critics. Today, modern Christians derive their knowledge of Christ to a large extent from his recorded encounters with other people thousands of years ago. Each parable, each individual gesture of love, and each healing combines to form a cohesive testament to what he was and still is to all people, even though he had direct contact with only a relative few.

Similarly, if we can accept the stories of the persons whose experiences with Christ are recounted in the following pages, we have an opportunity to derive hope from what is apparently happening in the lives of at least some individuals today. The mere fact that these momentous encounters occur at all might go a long way to deepen our commitment to living according to higher ideals—if not also to enhance our readiness to have such sacred encounters ourselves.

"I will not leave you orphaned;
I am coming to you."
John: 14:18

2

First Contact

"Be in communion with me."
M. M.

FEW OF US, REGARDLESS OF OUR RELIGIOUS beliefs, expect to meet Christ face-to-face during our lifetime. We assume that such things just do not happen to ordinary people, so a person's first encounter with Christ usually comes as quite a surprise. In these initial encounters, which I have called awakening Christ encounters, Christ's manifestation seems to revolve around the singular aim of inviting the recipient into a deeper relationship with him. Typically, the individuals who contributed awakening encounters were involved in spiritual study or seeking at the time, but were nonetheless startled when Christ himself appeared.

The initial encounter with Christ can be brief, a snapshot of what might become, in time, an ongoing experience of spiritual communion. However momentary, such awakening experiences leave the recipients yearning for a closer relationship with Christ, and yet feeling at the same time that the relationship already exists. Consider, for instance, the deep dream of B.S.

> *I have never had a dream like this one. In it, Jesus—so real, in living color—stood before me. As he came closer and closer I was about to put my head on his chest, but before I ever actually touched him, it ended. The emotional impact on me was tremendous. I was filled with a sense of total happiness and peace. It was as if every longing for love I had ever known was now totally satisfied. When it was over, I sat in bed a little disappointed at not having actually touched Jesus, but yet I was very contented. I went back to sleep, but I recalled that episode the moment I awoke, and it truly has been with me ever since. The years have dimmed the memory of the color a little, but the memory of the emotions have remained very keen. I believe I have had a little taste of what heaven will be like. (1st B.S.)*

As one might expect from such encounters, the experience almost always signals the beginning of a new phase in one's life, characterized by a greater sense of personal closeness with Christ.

The following experience was submitted by a woman who had reservations at first about whether she should share her Christ encounters in this book. In particular, she expressed concern that such accounts might awaken jealousy or a sense of inadequacy in people who have not experienced Christ in such a direct manner. Believing strongly that her own experiences came to fill a need at the time, she didn't want to imply that Christ comes to those who somehow deserve it. Even so, she eventually decided that the potential benefits of sharing her experiences with others outweighed any drawbacks.

My first experience was at night. I had been lying in bed praying. I was pulled away from praying by a light in the hallway outside my room. The light seemed to be coming from down the hall, outside my view. As I watched, the light grew brighter. It seemed to be coming down the hall toward my room.

Then I saw Jesus carrying a candelabra with seven lit candles. He was tall and dressed in a dark bluish-purple robe that had crescent moons and stars on it. The edge of the garment and sleeves were trimmed in gold.

He walked into my room, placed the candelabra on the floor, and knelt to pray by the side of my bed.

I moved my right hand and touched his hair.

I shall never forget the way his hair felt. I was engulfed with his love and the soft glow he and the candles brought to the room.

After a while, he picked up the candelabra and walked toward the door. As he walked through the doorway, I asked, "How can I reach you again?"

He turned and smiled. A warm, radiant smile that had an amused turn to it. His eyes danced playfully, lovingly.

"I'm in the phone book," he replied.

He turned and walked away while I found myself wondering how he would be listed in the phone book. How would I find him? And then I knew that he would be listed under "Emmanuel." When I looked Emmanuel up in the dictionary the next day, I discovered that Emmanuel means "God is present in the world." (M.L.P.)

An interviewer asked the great psychiatrist Carl Jung toward the end of his life if he believed in God. After a long pause, he answered, "I don't believe. I know. I *know*." Whether experience can or should ever fully take the place of faith, M.L.P. can say with a greater degree of certitude than ever before, "I *know*."

M.L.P.'s hesitancy to share her experiences is by no means unusual. Many of the individuals who submitted their accounts said that they had related their experiences to only one or two persons. The Christ encounter leaves a person feeling the need to remain silent, in many instances, to protect the sacredness of the experience. The woman who submitted this extraordinary encounter did so after years of remaining silent.

I was attending prayer vigil before evening daily Mass. When I got out of my car in the parking lot of Most Holy Trinity Church, I glanced at the clock and knew that the vigil would begin in a few minutes. Hurriedly, I approached the street corner and crosswalk. Stopping to look both ways, I was aware of a sudden dark deadness. I looked up over my left shoulder to see very large clouds forming. The wind blew strongly and I felt a storm approaching. I stopped to watch the quick buildup of clouds overtaking the eastern sky.

From behind the greatest dark cloud, which now appeared to me as a thunderhead, emerged the brightest light I've ever experienced. It filled the remainder of the sky and all about me. I felt short of breath. I could not move. I didn't want to miss this!

From out of this light and on top of the stationary "thunderhead" flowed liquid gold, as though it were being poured.

It built up and accumulated in height, from which the form of Jesus appeared.

(Words here seem inadequate to describe the experience. I still cry as I recall the whole experience again.)

I stood in awe and obedience before him. His robe was hooded and fell in soft folds about him. His facial features were not really distinct, but were there vaguely. The bright light and gold engulfed me also. I stared and waited.

From under his robe, the gold poured out forward and fell toward me and the parking lot, much like lava, slowly curving here and then there. As I watched, mentally I told myself that the Lord had come for me. "I am ready," I uttered softly. I felt such joy, such happiness, such excitement, yet my physical body remained very still. The golden path now was almost to the parking lot and about six to ten feet from where I stood. I left my body to meet the path. As I did, the gold stopped flowing. I heard the message, "Not now, listen." I stopped and listened intently, suspended.

"Be in communion with me." I could hear and feel his words. They filled every space within me and about me. Still outside myself and full, I watched as the gold "lava" went back upward to him and all form disappeared. I was back in my body before the light was gone.

Now my body shook all over. I couldn't settle it down or make it still. I felt confused, and I didn't know if I should go to my car or to prayers. I wanted to shout and jump and dance and cry and laugh with joy all at the same time.

When I entered the church, prayers were in process. I sat where I usually did, next to Sister Mary Damian, one of the leaders of our Tuesday prayer group. I shook noticeably, fumbling in my prayer book to find the correct prayer. I dropped to my knees in frustration and gratitude. "Damian," as we call her, helped me by sharing her book with me. I was never able to "get it together" before the service ended.

When I shared a piece of my experience with her, Damian said simply, "I know. It is so beautiful." I felt so full, full of love. Other than Sister Damian, I did not tell anyone about my experience for eight years, and then I shared it with my very close, spiritual friend. I felt that it was such a sacred experience that to tell it as I experienced it might lessen its value.

One thing was most clear. I needed to be in communion with our Lord and God. Increasingly, I walked a narrower path, with a knowing that surmounted logical reasoning. Trust increased. Discernment became clearer. Barriers melted. Surprises came. Meditation became more frequent. And I realized that being in communion with him means manifesting his love in fuller ways with others, as well as with myself, than I'd known before.

I pray for that direction and listen for his love in whatever way it may come. And then I await to know how best to pass that love on to others. It is a knowing, not a message in words. My attentiveness leads me in several directions.

It is time for me to share this experience. (1st M.M.)

M.M.'s experience is one of the most dramatic Christ encounters included in this book. We can sense how her devotion had established an opening through which Christ could reach out to her. And one can feel the tremendous love and authority emanating from the Christ as M.M. shows herself willing to surrender to him. While her encounter fits the criteria of an awakening encounter, it also includes instruction of a global nature. His admonition to her—to be in communion with him—leaves so much open-ended. His message seems to imply, Do whatever you must do to be in communion with me. While the goal is set by him, the methods are up to her. In the ensuing pages, the reader will discover again and again how *open-ended* Christ's messages are to the witnesses of his presence. Even though he wants, above all, a person's full commitment, he leaves it up to each person to decide how to accomplish this singular aim.

The awakening encounter, in particular, seems to leave a great deal unanswered. Christ appears briefly and powerfully, and then leaves the witness to contemplate the meaning of the experience thereafter. In this vein, a forty-one-year-old woman feels that she was called by Christ in her first encounter to involve herself in some form of spiritual work. Two years after her initial Christ encounter, she is still trying to define the deep sense of calling that was stirred to life by Christ's appearance.

I was in my bedroom preparing to go to bed when suddenly I saw a man in the doorway. He was dressed in white biblical-type robes and was surrounded by a golden glow. Even the folds of his robes seemed to reflect this golden light. He did not look like the pictures of Jesus that I've seen so often in churches. Instead he had shoulder-length dark hair and a beard. I could not clearly see his eyes, yet felt that they reflected a gentle nature. Not a word was spoken. When I first saw him, I was shocked. I told myself my eyes were playing tricks on me, so I closed them tightly and then opened them. He was still there. Again, I closed my eyes and again he was still there. Suddenly, he was gone.

I thought for sure I was going crazy, so I made an appointment to talk to a psychologist. I did not tell her what happened, just that there were some problems in my family and I wanted to be sure that I had not inherited any predispositions. She said I tested out fine, although I was showing some signs of stress. (J.F.)

J.F. was left feeling that she had been called by Christ. But to do what? Months after this first encounter, she dreamed of Christ again. This time, she saw him and a nun standing nearby, waiting for her. Again she was left with no clear direction. It is interesting that so many recipients of Christ encounters are left wondering what to do next. One might conclude that the Christ encounter is, as yet, unfinished, that additional installments will eventually complete the picture. It might be hard to believe that Christ would manifest to us only to leave us with more unanswered questions than before. But perhaps this is one purpose of the Christ encounter—to stir the individual to greater life through activating an impassioned, unceasing search for one's true calling.

An eighteen-year-old woman experienced Christ coming to her as she dreamed of drowning in her own baptismal waters. Like most awakening accounts, it is enigmatic and powerful, leaving so much unanswered.

About the time of my eighteenth birthday I dreamed one night that I was in a moonlit garden, and three angels appeared to me and asked if I wanted to be baptized. I said, "Yes," even though I wasn't sure I did. They led me to a very deep pool. I immediately became very scared because I didn't know how to swim, so I protested that I couldn't get into that pool because I might drown. They assured me that they would watch me and insisted that I go on in. I did, and immediately the water started whirling like a whirlpool, faster and faster. I was struggling with all my might to stay up but I kept getting sucked down. I looked up at the angels and they just leaned over the edge, expressionless. They watched me but made no move to help. The pool then seemed like a large deep well. Finally, I was so exhausted, I resigned myself to the idea that I was going to drown.

I looked up one last time and saw Jesus, dressed in a white robe. He reached down and extended his right hand, and I reached up with my right hand. I was immediately out of the pool and sitting beside him. I don't remember what he said to me.

I walked around in a kind of glow for weeks, but never told anyone about the experience. Finally, I suppressed it and forgot about it until years later. I've since told it several times when I've thought it was appropriate. (P.B.)

An interesting aspect of P.B.'s experience is the contrast between the angels, who remain dispassionate throughout, and Jesus, who reaches out to save her. While we can never discern the ultimate truths from our limited perspective, P.B. nonetheless perceived the angels as being unavailable to her in her time of need. Compassion arises from having shared similar experiences with the one who is in distress. Christ's capacity to reach out to us with compassion makes perfect sense because he lived and suffered as one of us. And so underlying P.B.'s experience is the belief, if not the fact, that the support she needs can only be found in one who lived and suffered in the world and can understand the struggles that she faces.

If we knew more about each witness, we would probably conclude that most awakening Christ encounters are healing experiences as well, which address a particular dimension of either the individual's unresolved past or problematic present. The following account comes across as a classic awakening encounter. It does not directly address a problem in need of healing. However, when questioned further, the individual was able to see that the content of the experience was tailor-made to heal the effects of her emotional abuse as a child.

> *My experience happened in the 1960s during a period of time in which I was seeking.*
>
> *At the time, I was visiting Yellowstone National Park. I had a dream that I was in my own apartment and there was a knock at the door. I opened the door and Jesus stood there. It was all light. He opened his garment and showed me his heart, which appeared to me as a bright light. He motioned for me to come closer and I saw there were actually two hearts that were joined and interlocking. I'm usually shy and very reserved, but I did not feel that way during the experience.*
>
> *When I woke up I felt wonderful, for I found that he really existed.* (R.J.)

When R.J. was asked about her association to the two hearts, she said, "I think it pertained to love. I was an unwanted and abused child and had never experienced love. I had to learn love. I believe that one of the hearts was his and one mine." She went on to say that she believed the experience meant for her "to become one with him and love everybody."

In a great many of the Christ encounters included in these chapters, the appearance of brilliant light serves as a prelude to Christ's personalized manifestation. Innumerable spiritual contemplatives—both Christian and otherwise—have observed the connection between the interior experience of white or golden light with the highest spiritual states. In Raymond Moody's *Life After Life*[16] and other studies of the near-death experience, the being who appears to the dying person is almost always surrounded by or bathed in light. And sometimes the dying person sees only an orb of light which, nonetheless, is felt to be a being who loves the person in an unconditional way.

If any experience can be considered the core mystical experience, the occurrence of brilliant white light is the obvious candidate. In support of the centrality of the white light experience, Carl Jung said:

> *The phenomenon itself, that is, the vision of light, is an experience common to many mystics, and one that is undoubtedly of the greatest significance, because in all times and places it appears as the unconditional thing, which unites in itself the greatest energy and the profoundest meaning.*[17]

The Secret of the Golden Flower

Could it be that those persons who come from non-Christian backgrounds are more likely to experience Christ in a less personified, radiant form? A Jewish woman, who respects all religions as well as her own Jewish faith, experienced Christ coming to her on the rays of the morning sun.

I have been meditating for thirteen years. Even though I was born into the Jewish faith and still actively practice Judaism, I am open to all religions and believe in the unity of all people. I also attend the monthly Unity Church meetings because I love singing praises to God. I also write nondenominational devotional hymns. I have allowed myself to be open to Jesus' teachings of spreading love and becoming enlightened.

One morning while I was meditating before sunrise, I felt the sun rising in the east as it began to shine through the window. The sun filled my heart with such warmth that it spread throughout my being. As I was filled with this warmth, I felt Jesus arising from the sun within me and spreading his arms wide. Love spread over me and I heard him say to me, "I am the Way."

This occurred as an internal experience: My eyes remained closed. It was very real, however, for the warmth and love brought such peace to my being.

What it meant to me, though, might be different than to a Christian. I felt it to be the true essence of Jesus' teachings—that we can all reach complete harmony with God, as did Jesus. I did not feel that I was to become Christian—but I was to know that Jesus is that pure love, and God is that pure love, and that we are all meant to grow to become one with all creation.(L.W.)

It is perhaps significant that L.W.'s encounter with a radiant Jesus did not push her in the direction of becoming a Christian. Rather, it deepened her convictions about the universality of Jesus' message and how it transcends doctrinal, even religious boundaries.

One might expect non-Christians to experience Christ as a universal being or impersonal force to whom they can relate within their own religious traditions. But from the following, we can see that this is not always the case. In A.Z.'s experience, Jesus appeared and identified himself to the witness.

Following my graduation from high school, I had my first "mind-blowing" experience which shook me to the core. I was living in Palo Alto with a number of young men my age while we participated in a sort of live-in encounter group. Needless to say, it was an emotionally intense and stressful time.

One night I had a profoundly numinous dream of my being in a dark, primitive room standing in the shadows against a wall which was lined with dark, aboriginal men. In the center of the room was a skylight in the shape of a Christian cross with brilliant sunlight streaming in at an angle from above, creating a brightly lit cross on the dirt floor. I moved toward the light, looked back to where I had been standing, and saw a Madonna-like figure swathed in colorful glowing robes.

I stepped into the light, looked up into it, and suddenly the whole dream exploded into an ineffable sensation of electrical energy cascading through my whole being. White light as bright as the sun poured through me, eliminating what felt like membranes or veils in the process. The face of Jesus appeared just in front of me against the background of bright white light and a voice said, "I am Jesus." I became aware of what felt like my face turning to stone and cracking, and the face in front of me began fracturing.

The whole episode ended just as abruptly as it began, and I was left in my bed sobbing in fear and quaking uncontrollably for about fifteen minutes. I had absolutely no idea

through the oak trees

of what hit me, but it was not of this world. It was more real
than anything I had ever experienced, and it was indescrib-
ably powerful.

Having been raised in a household with a Hindu father
and a spiritually "neutral" mother, I was unprepared to
deal with why the image of Jesus, of all people, should come
to me in such a profound way. (A.Z.)

We can sense just how foreign these experiences can seem
when they don't fit into our beliefs. Like Saul's encounter with
Jesus on the road to Damascus, the experience can be literally shat-
tering; for everything that we once held to be true is threatened by
the overwhelming authority of the encounter. We can't deny the
experience, but we can't integrate it either, at least at first. It seems
especially significant that the figure said—as he did to Saul—"I am
Jesus," not "I am Christ."

Given his upbringing, A.Z. may have found it comparatively
easy to incorporate a vision of a cosmic Christ into his spiritual
framework, for Christ is sometimes regarded as the essential
spiritual nature of Jesus the man. But the being did not make it easy
for A.Z. to identify him as only a universal presence or force—he
asserted his humanness as well. Consequently, A.Z. will no doubt
have to deal with the man Jesus one way or the other—if not to accept
his place in his life, then to argue eloquently for his exclusion.

While the experience of radiance is one of the hallmarks of the
classic near-death experience, this next near-death experience
featured a very human Jesus without the accompanying radiance.
This Christ encounter occurred when a young, pregnant
Englishwoman contracted tuberculosis and became so ill that she
was temporarily declared clinically dead.

Although it happened years ago, it is as fresh in my mind as if it were yesterday. I was in the hospital and very ill, having contracted tuberculosis at work. We had been testing a herd of cattle for the tuberculosis virus, and the pregnant cows came down with the disease. As I was also pregnant, so did I. Subsequently, I became so ill that I was pronounced dead at one point, and had a near-death experience before I was "sent back" to continue my life.

During the experience, I saw lots and lots of steps leading up to a building. I'd gotten about halfway up when I was stopped by a man. He wore no white robe, nor did he have wings. This man was so lovely, but there was so much sorrow in his face, so much suffering, as if for all of mankind. He also expressed so very much love and compassion. I felt he knew all about me and loved me; but he told me I couldn't go any further as I still had so much work to do.

This man wasn't white or black, but he had very bronzed skin as if he had been living out in the open and had been in the sun a lot. He wore a robe which I would say was homespun or handwoven. He wore sandals that were just soles with a strap over the big toe. He seemed dusty and weary, but so loving. I have now come to feel that what I saw was the real Jesus.

Afterward, I began searching to know and find everything I could about him—not just what is in the Bible. I was exposed to that as a child and, although I can now read it with a little more understanding, I have been looking for more.

My earth time is coming to an end and apart from missing the family, I am looking toward going back home.

I just hope I can continue to cope with the pain, and not be too much a burden to others. I have arthritis, angina, arteriosclerosis, and have had seven major operations—one for cancer, which I now feel is coming back. As he said, I had work to do; but I now understand he also meant work on myself! (K.V.D.)

Obviously, K.V.D. has deeply integrated her experience with Christ into an attitude toward living and dying, which is both realistic and fearless. We might hope that her encounter with Christ would have saved her from undergoing the obvious suffering that she still faces. But it's possible that the very illnesses that have plagued her have promoted a deeper, more fearless orientation to life. I am reminded of Ralph Waldo Emerson, who was once approached by a man who told him that the end of the world was imminent. Emerson calmly replied, "I can live without it." One gets the sense that K.V.D., too, is a person who can live meaningfully with or without the security that many of us take for granted.

K.V.D.'s account clearly satisfies the definition of a near-death experience (NDE) as well as the definition of a Christ encounter. Physical trauma, or temporary clinical death, is clearly one way to have an encounter with Christ prior to our final departure from this world.

Some people, however, seem to have the capacity to enter this state of communion without suffering the attendant physical trauma of a near-death experience. For example, the following dramatic out-of-body experience ushers B.S. into an initially lonely, but ultimately fulfilling, encounter with Jesus.

In the fall of 1979, when my husband and I were heavily involved in Christian ministry and very happy in what we were doing, I began to have a lot of out-of-body experiences. Finding little Christian-oriented literature that dealt with the experience in a positive manner, I chose to claim Jesus' protection and set about to learn all I could from these things on my own. I realized that much scriptural revelation has come from such experiences, and I had a deep hunger to know God in a more direct, personal sense.

One night while I had been sleeping, I became aware of the sensation of leaving my body behind and traveling at a great rate of speed to a series of localities where I seemed to be observing fields of crops in various stages of cultivation. There seemed to be modern equipment, such as tractors. This surprised me, as it seemed as if I'd been hopping from one primitive island to another and didn't expect to see a lot of modern equipment. Even though I saw houses, I became more and more disturbed that there were no people.

Finally, I was set down in a lonely, isolated area that I sensed was the backyard of my childhood home. However, there were no buildings in sight, and I felt totally abandoned.

Usually, my experiences in the out-of-body state were a time of learning. I could usually grasp the "lesson." But this time I didn't understand, so I asked God to show me what it was all about. When I received nothing, I began to challenge him, and reminded him about his promise of wisdom to anyone who asked: "If any of you is lacking in wisdom, ask God, who gives to all generously and ungrudgingly, and it will be given you" (James 1:5). I also reminded him that he wasn't supposed to be a "respecter of persons," and if he could manifest himself to others in dreams and visions, he should be willing to do that for me, too. I began to feel frustration, resentment, rejection, and finally a deep sense of despair.

Several times I tried to return to my sleeping body, but could not. Then, after totally despairing, I felt some intense <u>vibrations</u> and a high-pitched tone. It was almost as if some sensitive electronic equipment was being tuned. The vibrations were emanating from behind me and I felt the presence of someone whom I perceived to be Jesus. Embarrassment and shame at having railed at him competed with my desire to turn around and see him face-to-face.

My great desire to "behold him as he is" won out and I turned—but I didn't see him. Oh well, *I thought,* I knew he wouldn't be there. *Disappointed, and feeling self-justified, I returned to my self-pity and despair.*

Suddenly, there it was again, the vibrations that I knew emanated from him. This time, knowing that he would be there, I turned quickly around. He—Jesus—was just stepping out from behind a large tree.

"You don't look like you're supposed to look," I told him. I was surprised that his hair was so much lighter than I had visualized him to have. His eyes were almost green. He was laughing at me with his eyes, much as one who is amused by a small but stubborn child.

"I've been here all along," he said. "Blessed are those who have not seen and still believe."

Overwhelmed by a sense of unworthiness and disloyalty, I fell to my knees in repentance before him. "Oh, Lord," I cried, "I'm so sorry that I ever doubted you." He was standing directly in front of me, and I reached out to hold him around the knees. I remember thinking that I knew I was having a vision of Jesus, which was wonderful. But, of course, I knew that I wouldn't be able to feel anything but air when I tried to touched him. But as my arms went around his knees, I was astounded. There was substance there! I was having flesh and blood contact with the man Jesus himself.

Again, I sensed his amusement as he reached down and lifted me to my feet. Vibrations or waves of unconditional love and forgiveness flowed from him around me and into my being.

Then putting his arm around me, we began to walk together. He started to explain some things that I needed to know. He started to say, "In the central ocean are 7,000 to 8,000 islands. . . ." But as I listened, the words faded out, even though there seemed to be so much that he taught me. The next thing I knew, I was returning to my sleeping body, and I awoke.

Several years later, I met someone who thought the part about the central ocean was a restatement of Jesus' words, "In my Father's house are many mansions." (2nd B.S.)

B.S.'s experience is as sobering as it is uplifting. She exhibits all of the impatience and loss of faith that might befall any spiritual seeker who, after trying everything to get closer to God, gives in to angry despair when God does not appear willing to make good on his promises. But no matter how much anger and frustration she expresses, Christ still comes to her. His love overlooks those qualities that might otherwise render her unacceptable to any ordinary person. One gets the feeling that her attitude had little, if any, impact on his profound regard for her, even though it might have delayed somewhat his making himself known to her.

Jesus' willingness to make himself known to B.S., in spite of her lack of patience and faith, is consistent with the way he appeared to others who eventually served him so well. For instance, Teresa of Avila spent years fighting her spiritual calling, wishing instead to pursue the secular lifestyle of a wealthy, attractive woman. During this struggle, she suffered from a strange disorder which rendered her paralyzed and in extreme physical pain for days on end. This disorder was apparently due to her resistance to God's calling; for once she submitted fully to her spiritual life, her symptoms disappeared and Jesus thereafter appeared to her regularly for many years.

We can see from these moving experiences that the awakening Christ encounter typically takes the recipient by surprise, even in those rare cases in which the individual actually sought the experience beforehand. It conveys the impression that Christ *alone* is making the experience happen, that he is taking the initiative to introduce himself for the apparent purpose of bringing into our awareness a relationship that he *already* recognizes. We can sense, as well, that our beliefs, resistances, and fears pose insignificant obstacles to his love for us.

> "... *I will come again and will take you to myself,*
> *so that where I am, there you may be also.*"
> John 14:3

3

Healing
and Consolation

"I promise you it won't hurt. Turn over."
Laura

TWO THOUSAND YEARS AGO JESUS BECAME KNOWN
to people largely through his miracles of healing. Some of the most
moving passages in the gospel record, those which instill faith in the
reader during the most hopeless times, concern those instances
when Jesus relieved the pain, suffering, or lifelong disabilities of the
people who came to him for help. His willingness to save his friends
and acquaintances from illness, suffering, and even death shows us
just how much he cared to minister to the human and spiritual
needs of those he loved.

Many of these accounts suggest that this healing ministry still
goes on. The stories in this chapter concern Christ encounters
which occurred when the recipients or their loved ones were facing
a physical or medical crisis. Because these experiences involve

specific physical conditions and events, they serve to remind us that the Christ encounter can effect changes in the most concrete dimensions of a person's life. Some readers may find it easier to accept the validity of other accounts which do not produce measurable results once they see that Christ encounters can, at least in some instances, result in dramatic physical changes.

Physical Illness and Healing

As we have seen in the previous chapter, some persons experience Christ as a radiant, less personified being, while others perceive him as a very human Jesus. And some recipients have experienced Christ in both ways. For instance, M.L.P.—a woman whose very personal encounters with Jesus appear in other chapters—also had a healing encounter with a "shining stranger" who, despite his indistinct appearance, loved her enough to heal her with his tears.

> *I was going through a stressful time and had an excruciating headache. It was so bad, in fact, that I had wrapped my head in my dark cashmere sweater to try to keep out the light which seemed to hurt my head. My face was uncovered. I had been writhing on the bed, apparently, because I was lying crosswise on the bed, with my head toward the east. The pain was so bad that I felt tears in my eyes. Then I realized that someone was standing at my head and when I opened my eyes I saw a "shining stranger" bathed in light. He was crying and the tears that fell from his eyes were dropping on my eyes, causing tears that I had thought were my own. In a type of out-of-body experience, I felt myself leave my body and turn to face him. We embraced and together began turning and ascending in a type of dance of mystical union. (M.L.P.)*

If M.L.P. had never experienced a more distinct Christ, we might speculate on the identity of this "stranger." But having known her for many years, I also know that her relationship with Christ is the central truth in her life. Why he appeared in such an indistinct way is simply beyond our knowing, but perhaps it was because the spiritual union that ensued had to be experienced less personally, and less physically as the union we experience in our physical relationships.

Regardless of his indistinctness, his love was profoundly felt. His tears indicate that he suffered with M.L.P., even as he healed her.   *com - passion (suffer with)*

The following account involves a two-stage process in which the recipient was first apparently healed of a physical condition, then shown the source of the healing in a dramatic waking vision days later. The being is more clearly defined than in M.L.P.'s experience, but retains some its indistinctness. Here is the experience in A.D.'s own words:

> *I fell down a flight of stairs and was injured so badly that my lower spinal column was in almost continuous distress and pain. I had frequent chiropractic treatments for it. Getting in and out of bed became a careful process, and I would be somewhat stiff in the morning getting up. Even so, I rose at 6:30 A.M. for meditation (because it was the least interrupted, quiet time for me) and to prepare breakfast for my husband and children.*
>
> *This was the pattern of my life for seven years. One evening, my husband stayed up to watch a late TV sports review and I went to bed. I had just changed into my nightgown when I sensed a presence standing close beside me,*

on my left, and a (male) voice said, "This night sleep on your stomach, Alice." The voice that spoke my name was as clear and normal as when two persons are in conversation.

I started to protest in a gentle way. "But you know I can't sleep on my stomach!" I said with mock alarm, meaning that my back would become so rigid in the night that I would need help to get out of bed. Yet even as I said this, I obeyed quietly as a child would, and remembered thinking how astonishing that I could do this, and fell into deep sleep in this manner almost immediately.

Later, in reliving this extraordinary scene in my mind (and I did many times), I recall how amusing it seemed to me—as I was speaking the words—that I would remonstrate with a spiritual being! It still does. It is recounted here as it happened to illustrate how natural the entire incident seemed.

In the morning, just before actually waking, I distinctly felt the touch of hands massaging, manipulating, and pressing lightly on the lower region of my back. I slipped out of bed as though there had never been an injury.

For three full days I was in a silent, prayerful state filled with awe and reverence, consumed with wonder. Whose hands did I feel on my back? Who was it that healed me?

On the third night, I went to bed a little earlier again. As I closed the door, the entire wall facing me disappeared, and where there had been a large window and tall furniture occupying that wall space, there was now a brilliant panel of light. I stood transfixed, gazing at it. In the center was a figure in full height, with his hands outstretched, palms upward. He was showing me how my back was healed and *who had healed me. I say "he" because I knew instinctively it was the voice I had heard earlier, but this time no words were exchanged. The figure appeared to be neither male nor female, nor were the hands characteristic of either. The face was so luminous I could not make out the features, but the hair was plainly visible. It glistened with soft brown waves and fell to the shoulder. He wore a single white garment with no apparent seams, reaching from the neck to the floor and covering the feet, with full, open sleeves at the wrist.*

He stood like this for several seconds, and then the wall reappeared in the fraction of a moment as inexplicably as it had disappeared moments before. I remained in that state of grace for some time afterward, and even today, more than thirty years later, the event is indelibly etched in my mind and very simple to recall in all its detail.

Since that first remarkable experience, I have received three other instantaneous spiritual healings. . . . More than anything, it has nurtured in me the concept of gratitude. (A.D.)

The experience of physical healing would have been life-changing all by itself. But then to be shown that the agent of healing was a radiant being who cared enough to reveal "himself" to A.D. must have curtailed any tendency to explain away the remarkable change as a coincidence. It is as though the Being appears not just to satisfy A.D.'s curiosity but to leave no doubt in her mind about the source of her healing.

It is interesting to note that A.D. actually had to *do* something for the healing process to occur. Some physical effort on her part was required. This requirement is reminiscent of Jesus' manner of healing in the gospels. He would sometimes require supplicants to perform some physical action as part of the healing process. For example, in John 9:1–11 we find the story of Jesus' healing of a man who was born blind. Jesus mixed his own spittle with soil to make clay. Then he placed the clay over the man's eyes and gave him a task: Go to a specific pool and wash off the clay. Only when the man did this was he healed.

On another occasion, Jesus told ten lepers that he would heal them. Before the healing could take place, he told them to present themselves to the priest so that their miraculous healing could be duly acknowledged, according to the Jewish tradition. The healing took place only as they were on their way to see the priest:

> *When he saw them, he said to them, "Go and show yourselves to the priests." And as they went, they were made clean. Then one of them, when he saw that he was healed, turned back, praising God with a loud voice. He prostrated himself at Jesus' feet and thanked him* (Luke 17:14–19).

Of course, we are left to wonder in each of these situations, was the specific action necessary to complete the healing process? Or was it one of many possible tests of the person's willingness to act on faith? A.D. had to be willing to assume a sleeping posture that had previously been painful to her, not knowing for sure if any good would come of it. In essence, Christ required her to take a leap of faith before the healing could take place.

The same requirement can be found in the story of Laura, which was recounted in Chapter 1. She, too, was asked to do something that had previously been excruciating—to turn over in bed and face Jesus. Other aspects of her story parallel the most dramatic New Testament examples of Jesus' healing ministry.

Indeed, Laura's miraculous recovery from terminal spinal meningitis reverberates with the faith-inspiring force of some of the most dramatic gospel accounts of healing. Her experience calls to mind the seemingly hopeless case of Jairus's daughter, whose situation appeared hopeless by the time Jesus arrived to minister to her, but who was nonetheless revived from apparent death (Mark 5:23–43). After Jesus told her parents that she was only sleeping, he took her by the hand and called to her, and she arose. We are also reminded of Jesus' own friend, Lazarus, who was resurrected by Jesus after being dead for some time.

Whereas the previous contributors in this chapter received physical healing for themselves during their Christ encounter experiences, another woman witnessed Christ healing her mother. This account exemplifies the mediating role that individuals can apparently play through prayer, belief, and love.

K.M.'s experience took place when she was twenty-five years old, when her mother was suffering from advanced stages of cancer.

As a child, I used to collect pictures of Jesus and hide them in a box of "treasures." My favorite was one of him on the cross. My aunt used to take me to the Methodist Church for Sunday school when I was four, five, and six. Except for that, I had no real religious background. But I've always believed very sincerely that Christ was there if I needed him.

I elected to be baptized at the age of twelve, and my dear aunt was the only person (besides the minister) present. Her faith was her beauty, though outwardly she was not beautiful.

Since both of my parents worked, I was very independent, and was never really close to my mother. But I loved her dearly, even though I felt that she was very detached from us all, and never really wanted me; I just "happened" to her. Mom and Dad fought often, and I was always throwing myself in the middle. Often alcohol was to blame, and on my mother's day off from work, she would often get drunk.

After I had graduated from college and was teaching high school English, my mother had her first cancer operation, a mastectomy. She underwent chemotherapy, but the prognosis was not good since she had the tumor for over a year without doing anything about it. After a second operation to remove her lymph nodes, her outlook was dismal. However, I was determined that I could save her life through prayer and calling on Christ for help.

I prayed desperately for his help and even offered to trade places with her. I would cry myself to sleep while praying. One night, I awoke about 3:00 A.M. and sat up. Somehow, my dear sleeping husband and I had been transported in our bed into my mother's bedroom, where she lay sleeping. I became aware that Christ was in the doorway, as if he hadn't just arrived, but had always been there. I was in awe, and felt part of a dramatic play, like an actor, and yet a member of the audience, too—watching, waiting, holding my breath.

The room grew bigger in size and clearer as Christ moved toward my mother's bed. The light was so intense— like sun glinting on the crystals of newly fallen snow—that it hurt my eyes to look, and I realized that part of that pain was my grief for my mother. Silently, gracefully, he walked or glided to her bedside and touched the side of her face, and then turned and nodded. He gazed at me, acknowledging me, and left through the same door.

*I woke up and it was morning. For the first time, I was
at peace knowing that Christ had intervened for my mother
and that she would live. I told my mother and father about
this years later, but somehow I don't feel that they believed in
its validity.*

But Mom is still alive today. (K.M.)

This story presents us with a dilemma as we try to understand
what happened. K.M. showed a deep love for her mother, and a
willingness to offer herself as a sacrifice for a woman who had given
her little in the way of love when she was a child. It would be easy
to interpret her attempts as unhealthy, or "codependent."

And yet this rather clinical assessment is stood on its head by
the consequences of K.M.'s loving intercession. Obviously,
whatever interpersonal problems existed between K.M. and her
mother posed an insignificant obstacle to the healing that ensued.
This surprising result simply shows how difficult it can be to distin-
guish between unhealthy self-sacrifice on the one hand, and on the
other, a gift of the highest form—giving one's life for another
person.

This distinction may ultimately be impossible to make from the
outside; for what appears to one person as a reasonable sacrifice to
make in a relationship may appear unhealthy to someone else.
Certainly, one cannot say that Jesus was "taking care of his own
needs" as he consented to mistreatment, suffering, and martyrdom.
He was operating from an entirely different viewpoint, one that
regarded the substitution of his own suffering for that of others as a
much more important concern than his own personal needs.

Is it unhealthy for us, as ordinary individuals, to take on
someone else's suffering? Charles Williams, English novelist and

philosopher, thought not. Indeed, he made the "law of substitution" the centerpiece in his interpretation of the spiritual path. He believed that the highest form of love was to take another person's suffering onto oneself, just as Jesus did.

> *We are to love each other as he loved us, laying down our lives as he did, that this love may be perfected. We are to love each other, that is, by acts of substitution.*[18]

One of the most beautiful and touching examples of apparent substitution is the case of Williams' friend and famous Christian writer, C. S. Lewis. He married late in life to Joy, who was suffering from cancer that had metastasized to her bones. Lewis loved Joy so much that he prayed to share her suffering. Soon after, her disease went into a remission that lasted two years, and Lewis began to develop severe osteoporosis—a rare condition for a man.

> *During the period of Joy's recovery he too contracted a bone disease, and although it was not malignant and was soon brought under control he was obliged to live carefully. "I wear a surgical belt and shall never be able to take a real walk again," he told a friend, "but it somehow doesn't worry me. The intriguing thing is that while I (for discoverable reason) was losing calcium from my bones, Joy, who needed it more, was gaining it in hers."*[19]

Lewis and K.M. demonstrated, perhaps, that there is no error attached to sacrifices made in the context of such deep abiding love. In one sense, such love is always potentially, if not actually, "self-destructive"; for *giving* life, rather than preserving one's own, becomes the paramount concern.

The distinction between physical and emotional healing breaks down in some of the Christ encounters that we have already considered. Certainly M.L.P.'s headache was prompted by more than physical imbalances, but she did not elaborate on the sources of stress that gave rise to her symptoms. Similarly, the next account reveals a woman in the throes of a spiritual crisis, during which she became deathly ill. Clearly, the problem reaches into all levels of her life, and the solution—Christ's admonition to reach out to others, in spite of their lifestyles—healed her on all levels, including the physical.

I grew up in the 1950s and 1960s in a home that could be characterized as traditional in many ways, and yet, at the same time, was dysfunctional. My father was an atheist; my mother, while not particularly religious, was a good woman who considered rearing her children in the church part of her duty as a good mother. We went to a Methodist church; however, from the age of seven on, I often went to the Catholic church with my girlfriend. I enjoyed the time of quiet prayer and the deep feeling of reverence I experienced there.

As far back as I can remember, I had always been in love with Jesus; I considered him my best friend. My father was an alcoholic, and there was often a great deal of turmoil and trauma associated with his drinking. I often escaped from the more stressful episodes by going outside and climbing on the roof, which I reached from the "dust porch" balcony on our second floor. It was there I developed a personal relationship with Jesus. I would talk to him and feel his presence, in a warmth that would surround me even on the coldest nights.

As most young people eventually do, I explored other faiths as I grew older. I spent many years involved in the study of Eastern mysticism and other "New Age" thought, but I eventually rejected this line of thinking, because I learned by way of a personal tragedy that evil is no illusion. Still, I had a hard time accepting many things in the Bible, and was not impressed with many of those who claim to be Christians. My spiritual life became a void that I filled by getting involved in community theatre. The close personal relationship I had with Jesus as a child still eluded me; I spent many bitter tears lamenting what I perceived as his "abandonment" of me.

In 1988 I was involved in a production of a play I had written that was being produced for a community charity. I became very close friends with two of the actors chosen for the play. They were an unusual couple. They claimed to be "born-again" Christians. They were a gay male couple. They had been together, at that time, seventeen years, and came to their faith within weeks of each other. What was most unusual about them was that they did not attend the churches that would support them in their lifestyle. They, in fact, disapproved of those churches for having bad doctrine. They believed every word of the Bible was true and did not shy away from the parts that would seem to condemn their lifestyle. They simply believed that God wasn't through with them yet; that their being gay was "the least of their sins." Because of their unique stand, they found themselves in the peculiar and painful position of being rejected by both the church and those in the gay/lesbian community.

My friends, Ian and Jim, had a profound effect on my life. They became my closest allies and friends. Ian and I formed a close spiritual bond. He had a way of talking about

God's plan that was sheer poetry, like the scriptures themselves, which came alive when he read from them. It didn't take long for me to remember the Jesus I had known as a child and to long for him again.

One night, when I was waiting for dress rehearsal to begin, something happened to me that I have since referred to as my born-again experience. I was standing outside in my "Aphrodite" costume (God does have a sense of humor), when a wind came from nowhere and time seemed to stand still. I heard a voice say to me, "I am coming, and you are naked." I knew the voice was Jesus. And I knew, at that instant, that this was the same voice that spoke to me when I was a child.

I never wanted to be without him again, and I committed my life to him on the spot.

After that night, I did what one would expect of a "new" Christian. I burned my New Age books and paraphernalia; I began to study the Bible, especially the Old Testament prophets. Things I had never understood before opened up to me in a way that was deeper, more fulfilling and exciting than anything I had ever experienced in the New Age circle.

And then I hit a crisis in my newfound "fundamentalism"—the problem of Ian and Jim, whose faith had led me back to Jesus in the first place. I had never met anyone with a stronger faith and love for Jesus as these two men. I knew Jesus loved them, and I was sure that their faith was pleasing to God. But many of the people I was now meeting in my attempts to find a church did not share my conviction.

Because I often elected to spend time studying with Ian and Jim, rather than those in the church, I came under personal attack from a number of well-meaning folks. One man was particularly relentless. He told me I was being deceived and would be pulled "under" with them.

He challenged me. He said that if I really wasn't under their influence, I would prove it by spending time away from them.

I wanted desperately to be pleasing to God; and I became confused about the issue of deceit. In my heart, I knew that Ian and Jim were genuine, but I decided I would do what the man suggested, in order to prove I loved God more than my friendship with Ian and Jim.

I didn't want to hurt them, so I didn't tell them why I wouldn't see them. I made up excuses. And I knew that they were probably sensing what was really going on. I moved from the apartment I was living in at the time and isolated myself.

Shortly after this, I became very ill—almost to the point of death—with the same virus that killed Jim Hensen. I was so ill that I didn't get out of bed for several weeks. I missed Ian and Jim, who, I knew, would have been there for me. I felt guilty over betraying our friendship. I cried out to Jesus to help me understand. That's when he came to me.

My encounter could be characterized as a "lucid dream," that is, one in which I knew I was dreaming during the dream. I felt and experienced everything in the dream as though it were really happening.

I was "transported" to the shore of a sea of quicksand. There were all these people in the quicksand crying out for someone to pull them out. I wanted to go in and rescue them, but every time I would start to, these voices behind me would yell out, "Don't go—it's a trick of Satan—they will pull you under with them."

As I hesitated, a white-robed figure came walking past me. His stride was grand and purposeful. It was Jesus. What he looked like isn't important; I knew it was him because he was the way I had always imagined him. He walked right into the quicksand and extended his hand to one of the people who was trying desperately to keep from sinking. Then, he turned and looked at me. I shall never forget that look. I still have the same emotional reaction whenever I remember this part. The way he looked at me said many things at once. It was a look that conveyed disappointment, compassion, and love. It was a look that said, "Gayle, Gayle, Gayle, when will you ever trust me?" The look also conveyed sadness that I had allowed the voices to keep me from helping the people who were crying out to me. And also, there was gentle admonishment. Then he motioned with his free hand for me to come in and join him in pulling the people out.

I was so overcome with emotion from this experience that I stayed up all night. The next morning I wanted to go and see Ian and Jim and tell them I was sorry. I was still very ill, but I was determined to walk the three miles to their home. It took me several hours, as I was having a great deal of difficulty breathing.

When I arrived, Ian opened the door and greeted me as though there had never been a rift between us. They both welcomed me and we sat down at their kitchen table. As I began telling them what I had done, I began sobbing uncontrollably—I asked them to please forgive me. The words weren't even out of my mouth when they both grabbed my hands and said, "There is nothing to forgive." The look in both of their eyes was the same look of compassion that Jesus had given me. At the moment our hands all touched, the fever and illness completely disappeared and I was healed.

This experience put to rest my doubts that may have lingered about Ian's and Jim's standing before God. Occasionally, when I meet a Christian who seems to be open, I have shared my encounter with Jesus.

Some of them have accepted the experience and have changed the way they relate to people who may share our faith but never reach the standard that we might impose upon them. Others have told me that I misinterpreted the dream, that Jesus was telling me that I should save these people from their lifestyle. But this wasn't the message that Jesus conveyed to me so clearly. He was telling me that there are many souls who long for him, who would gladly receive him if we reached out to them where they are. He was telling me that there are many who remain estranged from his love because his people have rejected them. And he was telling me that he has planted his heart within me, and I am to act on that love, and not the words of others.

We all struggle.

Looking back, I believe that God had a special purpose when he put Ian and Jim into my life in such a meaningful way. I later went on to work in the field I am currently engaged in, working with adults with developmental disabilities. It has been my experience that many of the caregivers in this field are of a gay and lesbian orientation. Most of these people have a deep yearning to know God. When they encounter Jesus, through me, they have not met with the rejection so many of them have experienced in

the past. They meet the Jesus I encountered on the shore of the
quicksand sea. (G.S.)

G.S.'s encounter with Christ suggests that by embracing Christ's inclusive love, we may tap into the greatest source of healing imaginable. Of course, most of us fall short of this ideal, and may consequently develop physical and emotional disorders that derive from the error of judging ourselves and others by a harsher standard than what Christ himself would apply. Perhaps we would do well always to consider the possibility that our illnesses may stem, at least in part, from a basic failure of loving ourselves and others—and to consider that our healing may lie in the inclusive spirit that Jesus exemplified in his walk among us.

G.S. remained a close friend with Ian until his death from cancer in early 2002. She wrote to me that Ian remained faithful and loving to the end, working tirelessly to bring people to Christ. She shared with me Ian's favorite hymn, an old Irish eighth-century hymn, that conveys so beautifully the sweetness of devotion that puts one's love of God above life itself.

Be Thou My Vision
An Eighth-Century Irish Hymn

Be Thou my vision, O Lord of my heart.
Not be all else to me save that Thou art.
Thou my best thought by day or by night,
Waking or sleeping, Thy presence my light.
Be Thou my wisdom and Thou my true word
I ever with Thee and Thou with me, Lord.
Thou my great Father, and I Thy true son,
Thou in me dwelling, and I with Thee one.

Riches I heed not, nor man's empty praise
Thou mine inheritance now and always
Thou, and Thou only first in my heart,
High King of Heaven, my treasure Thou art.
High King of Heaven, my victory won
May I reach Heaven's joys, O bright Heaven's son.
Heart of my own heart, whatever befall,
Still be my vision, O ruler of all.

Christ's Consoling Presence

In some encounters with Jesus, the recipients experience a remission of their symptoms, while in others they continue to decline. What makes the difference? Is it a person's virtue that, when combined with Christ's presence, unites to heal the body? If so, then those who go on to die would seem, by comparison, faulted in some way. Or could it be that those who die prematurely have, in some way, completed their mission and have been called by God to come home? Some have even said that death is not really the issue, it's how we live while we are here that matters in the mind and heart of God. Regardless, it is an age-old mystery why people have to suffer and die, often prematurely.

R.H. and his wife did everything they could to bring about her healing from cancer. In their search for medical alternatives they had joined a weekly study and meditation group. Eventually, as his wife grew weaker and weaker, the group began to meet at their home. Finally, she was so weak that she could only participate from her own bedroom while the rest of the members met in the living room. R.H. remembers:

At the close of one of our meetings, I went in to see my wife after all the other members had left. She looked radiant. I immediately asked her what had happened and she told me, "Oh, Jesus has just been here. He said that he'll come for me tonight at 3:00 A.M. Isn't it all wonderful?" She still seemed to be in an ecstatic state of joy. Such a statement of impending death seemed not to phase her a bit. I went on to bed in a separate room where I had been sleeping since her nights had become so restless with the illness. I set my alarm to wake me just before 3:00 A.M.

I was awakened at that hour and went in very quietly to her bedside, and sat down to watch her. At exactly 3:00 A.M. she stopped breathing and passed on. (R.H.)

Most of us experience a wide range of intense emotions when someone we love is suffering from a protracted and apparently terminal illness. Above all, perhaps, is a feeling of helplessness. Consequently, R.H. must have experienced a great deal of comfort knowing that Christ assisted his wife in her time of greatest need when he, himself, could do nothing. In that sense, the Christ encounter was for him, too.

The family of a terminally ill child also experienced consolation at a time when they were falling apart from the grief of his imminent death. Here is the account, told by the boy's older sister:

Cancer, the doctor said. March 15, 2001, changed all of our lives forever. At the center of all the raw emotion, the river of tears, was my little brother, Louie. Sixteen. How in the world could this happen? Why? No, no, no, no, not Louie.

We grew up in a modest household with plenty of commotion. Always a birthday party to celebrate, first communions, new births, graduations, and the endless seasons changing all of us rapidly, bringing us together yet again for another Christmas, another Thanksgiving, another Easter. At the core of every celebration there were Masses to go to, prayers of thanks, "rosarios" to remember, and blessings asked for by our elders, mostly for the Holy Spirit to keep us out of trouble! And blessed we all were. Twenty-five nieces and nephews, ten aunts and uncles, grandparents, great-grandparents, and cousins. Looking back now, we were really blessed, because for one moment in time that may have stretched for just a few short years, we were all together, alive, laughing, celebrating, enjoying the "now" of each and every day.

Like the fine silk threads that hold together a precious piece of cloth, our family began to unravel and grow apart. I strongly feel that it began with the death of my grandmother whom we all so lovingly grew up knowing as "t'Ama." This happened back in 1989, and for a few years we were closer than ever. And then differences surfaced and tensions grew from picking on old wounds to dwelling on faults and creating new ones.

When she died, Louie was only four years old. He didn't know her very well, but as he grew into a young man, he knew how important she had been. We remembered her on her birthday, the anniversary of her death, and kept her in our thoughts and prayers.

In March of 2001, Louie was diagnosed with Ewing's sarcoma, a form of rare, adolescent cancer. We had only six months to tell him how much we loved him, six months to tell him it would all turn out okay, only six months.

Louie was the type of person who loved to make a smart crack any chance he got. He was silly and always made us laugh. He loved music and was involved in his high school marching band. He also started a rock band with three of his buddies and it became his favorite pastime. He spoke of someday becoming a band director or designing fast, cool cars for some car company. He had just taken his tests to receive his driver's license, and was constantly pestering my dad for a new car. He had dreams like any other kid his age would have—and plenty of friends to live them out with.

It was during those six months that our whole family's faith was tested. Ironically, the minute we found out, my family began to heal. God had always been a part of us all, but never had we delved so deeply into what our faith really meant. Years of repetitive praying had become stale, like the glazed-over look a man gets when telling the same story to his children for the hundredth time. This new awakening allowed all of us to come together again. We prayed desperately for Louie's healing, sought answers to our deepest, most private questions, and awakened to a renewed and stronger faith.

Louie took all of this in stride. Although it was obvious that he was worried, his personality always shone through. His sarcasm was affectionate, making all of us laugh at his cleverness. This child we had taken for granted, thinking he would live to be an old man, accomplished more in those sixteen years than men three times his age could ever do.

My Grandfather, "Apa," a staunch believer in the saint Padre Pio, led us all to pray a rosary every night, asking special blessings for Louie. One afternoon my father, who was in the hospital room in San Antonio with Louie, received a call from his brother while everyone was gathered at our house in San Juan for the daily rosary. My uncle was running late for the rosary and had decided to make a quick call to my dad before going to our house, to see how Louie was doing that day.

Louie was lying in his hospital bed quietly, awake but with his eyes closed, when all of a sudden he felt a hand brush his forehead upward to the length of his head. He opened his eyes quickly and sat up on his bed. He says he thought it had been Dad, but Dad was still in deep conversation with my uncle and lying down on the bed by the window facing away from him. He waited until Dad got off the phone to ask if he had reached over to touch him while on the phone. Dad, puzzled, said he hadn't touched him.

Louie was adamant, saying over and over that someone had touched him—he had clearly felt a hand. Puzzled, my dad then called our house and spoke to one of my aunts. She said they had just finished praying and excitedly mentioned that they had asked Padre Pio for a sign that he was watching over Louie, that all of the prayers and rosaries they had been praying for two months straight were being heard by God. They had specifically asked for Padre Pio to put his hand on Louie's head not more than ten minutes prior. This sign of communication with Padre Pio confirmed that we were being heard, that Louie was not alone.

Weeks later, Louie awoke some time in the wee hours of the morning to a sight that many of us can only dream of— a sign from God.

Despite the constant reassurances from family, the abundance of prayers, and kind words and gestures, Louie had started to become emotionally distressed. He wanted to be home and pick up where he left off, going to school, making music with his band. Even doing homework sounded really good by this point. He just never imagined that it was going to get harder.

That night was like any other—machines beeping every hour, nurses constantly walking in and out. Louie told us that he awoke to the presence of a light shining from across the room. Its brightness was astounding, but not blinding. He says that as his eyes adjusted, he found that he was able to start making out words in a circular shape. They formed a circle spelling out "Always and Forever" with the word GOD right in the middle of the circle. What would have been the "O" in God was the Sacred Heart of Jesus. He says the writing was crooked, like the writing of a child. For a few minutes he tried to clear his eyes and attempted to wake my mother who slept just a few feet away. The whole time the image stayed in front of him and shone brightly. The following day he drew what he saw on a piece of paper and showed it to us.

We were amazed and felt like we had been given a gift. We wanted so much to believe that this meant he would be healed, that God would hear our prayers and give us a miracle.

In the end, Louie did pass away, but what we realized after the agony of our loss and the unimaginable pain was that our prayers had been answered. Having had him bless us with his presence for sixteen years, we were now able to see each other in a different light. Although it is hard to under-stand why this happened, we hold strong to the belief that he had finished his purpose for being here on earth, and that God had asked him to come back home.

Even though it feels like the world ended, the seasons continue their process of change, giving way to another Thanksgiving, another Christmas, and another Easter to celebrate. Meanwhile, we have found those unraveled threads in our family's cloth and have gently continued to "repair" them. The importance of family has never been stronger. We were so lucky to have had those six months to come together as a family, to forgive each other for things that are so petty in the end. It comes down to faith, family, and love.

The hurt is still fresh, some days are so much harder than others, but I know we will all be together again one day. Every day that's tucked away with the sun setting and our eyes closing is one day closer to being with him again. There's no doubt in my mind that he looks in on us every now and then. I can still hear his silly laugh and see his crooked little smile, and I'm sure he'll be the first one waiting to greet us when our time comes. His vision was a message to all who hear it, that no matter how uncertain, how scared we may be of the unknown, we must always see the blessing that is behind it. With faith nothing is unheard—in the end, it will be "Always and Forever, God."

While Louie's vision of Christ's presence did not heal him physically, it served to anoint him with Christ's love, and to unite his family in a deeper faith than ever before. While Jesus himself did not appear, the form in which the experience came was so clearly designed to appeal to a child's need for concrete reassurance, and to serve as an enduring emblem of Christ's love for his family.

Since most of us fear death and the loss of those we love, it might be hard to accept that Christ would manifest at all without actually reversing the illness which has befallen us or the one we love. We would like to have more than consolation—we would like for our loved ones to survive.

Perhaps we can look at it a different way. Maybe Christ comes principally to heal the spirit, not the body. Maybe, in some cases, the body responds also, and provides an additional healing effect. Given the fact that all of us are mortal, that death is imminent, maybe Christ comes to correct more serious conditions than illnesses and injuries. *Perhaps the primary focus for his healing is our need for love and hope.* Certainly, Christ's gift to Louie and his family brought immense healing on many levels, even though Louie eventually died.

Again and again history suggests that the Divine only rarely seems to alter the material conditions we face. And yet we can take heart that his love insulates us against the doubts and fears which prevent us from marshaling our best efforts in the face of adversity. Beyond that, it may also be true that he will assist us as he did for Louie—in the final transition from this world to the companionship he has promised.

I am the first and the last, and the living one.
I was dead, and see, I am alive forever and ever.
Revelation: 1:18

4

Healing the Heart

"Never be afraid because I will always be there with you."
L.H.

A SINGLE THEME UNIFIES THE OTHERWISE RICHLY diverse collection of Christ encounters presented in these chapters. Regardless of whatever else might take place, the Christ figure expresses *profound love* toward the recipient in every account. The way this love impacts a person seems to depend on his or her needs at the time. For instance, we have already seen that if a person is ill, the Christ encounter can promote actual healing—or at least confirm his love during a time of apparently unavoidable loss. As we'll see in the accounts that follow, the same intercessory process promotes mental and emotional healing if the person needs it. In a span of moments, the Christ encounter can lift a person out of emotional turmoil, leaving him free from paralyzing emotions and empowered to undertake new directions in life. The healing seems to take place as the witnesses recognize that they are loved and accepted by a radiant being who *knows them completely* and who points to a relationship with himself as a completely sufficient refuge for the "poor in heart."

The reader will observe in the following cases that an intensely personal relationship with Jesus develops in virtually every one. It is as though the emotional problems, often precipitated by inter-personal conflict or loss, could only be healed through a deeply personal connection to someone who *will never fail us.*

The Healing of Depression and Fear

Many of us have done something in our past that we cannot forgive ourselves for. The passage of time may take the edge off of our regret and even render it tolerable, but some of these memories remain largely untouched by time. No matter how many people around us try to alleviate our guilt and remorse, no matter how much we might try constructively to "reframe" our act in a way that makes it understandable, if not forgivable, we still hold ourselves accountable for something that apparently cannot be undone. What happens if we cannot forgive ourselves or accept the atonement available from our peers, our ministers, our counselors, or our society? The act becomes for us something that can be forgiven only through divine intervention, or "grace."

The experience of P.G. demonstrates how a Christ encounter can begin to usher a person beyond seemingly inescapable guilt and sorrow. The individual—who is today a thirty-two-year-old artist and mother of three—experienced a sense of deep healing after having an abortion at the age of nineteen.

About twelve years ago, circumstances seemed to force me into a corner and I made the decision to have an abortion, which devastated me. A couple days after the abortion, I went to an afternoon movie, trying desperately to run away from my thoughts. I ended up leaving the theater abruptly in the middle of the show and going for a drive into the country, crying and singing simultaneously "In the Garden." I became aware of a bright light filling the car. It was as if a huge flashlight was shining from above and the beam of bright light was following me down the road. I sensed the presence of Jesus so strongly sitting beside me that I kept looking for him in bodily form. When the light left, I felt calmed, restored, and forgiven. (2nd P.G.)

So many of us labor under the emotional consequences of actions that we cannot undo. P.G. experienced what is perhaps the only solution for such unrelenting regret—God's love for us anyway. C.M. faced a similar dilemma, except that the so-called "unforgivable" action was her father's suicide.

It is hard to imagine that, out of such a great tragedy as a parent taking his own life, great joy and peace can come, but that is what happened to me. At the age of fifty-seven, my father committed suicide by shooting himself in the head with his shotgun. I was at the funeral home and had just spent some quiet time with him before getting ready for the funeral itself. It was hard enough to lose my father, but to lose him in this way was almost more than I was able to stand. After the first shock of hearing what had happened, I was now trying to deal with what for me had come to be the hardest part. Because he had taken his life, I knew that he could not go to heaven. At least, this is what I had been taught, and it was hard to try to come to terms with that. I was struggling with this as I walked down the hall toward the chapel for my father's service. Just before I got to the chapel, a little voice that I now call my "knowing" said to look up, so I did.

There about six feet off the floor, floating toward the ceiling, was my father and Jesus Christ with their backs to me. They were hand in hand and seemed to be walking up and out the ceiling. As I looked at them, they turned their heads and both smiled at me. There was a bright light all around them, and there was the most wonderful feeling of love and peacefulness about them and in me. I knew at that moment that my father was going to be with God, and that he was happy and at peace. Then they disappeared in a fine mist.

I was able to go in to that service with a smile on my face and peace in my heart.

After this experience, I knew that what I'd been taught was wrong, and it would be up to me to seek out my own way to reach and serve God. (1st C.M.)

It is ironic that the very experience that releases C.M. from the belief that her father cannot be forgiven also precipitates a spiritual crisis for her: It forces her to go beyond her religious indoctrination to find her own path to God. Knowing the loneliness and interpersonal strife that can easily accompany such a personal journey, we can understand why individuals might unwittingly prefer not to encounter a being whose all-embracing love might compel them to question restrictive, but widely accepted, beliefs and doctrines. And yet it was this embracing love that repeatedly took Jesus beyond the social and religious customs of his day—a love that forgave prostitutes, that healed on the Sabbath, and that ultimately sought forgiveness for even those who killed him.

We can see this vast and boundless love operating in the experience of S.M., a hardened criminal who had clearly "made his bed in hell." At the lowest point of his life, Christ appeared, showing S.M. that none of us—not even a would-be killer—is beyond the reach of his love.

As a young child, I was sexually and physically abused by my real father, an alcoholic. After divorcing him, my mother remarried another alcoholic when I was about ten years old. He picked up where my father left off. So I ran away when I was fifteen years old and became a criminal.

I escaped from the Washington State penitentiary in 1970. One year to the day from my escape, the Oceanside Police Department had me hemmed in at a nightclub in downtown Oceanside. Being an escapee, and having just shot someone in a robbery in San Diego less than twenty-four hours before, I was desperate, to say the least. I hated blacks at the time, and knew I would kill a black if one ever got in my way.

I attempted to walk out the door of the nightclub past one of the police officers, who was a black man. He told me to halt. I kept walking. He told me again to halt! I could not have been more than fifteen feet from him. It was a bright, sunny day and I had no alcohol or drugs in my system. Other than being in a panic, my head was clear. In a split second, I made the decision to shoot him. Or, perhaps more accurately, maybe I made the decision to commit suicide.

I pulled a thirty-eight caliber from under my jacket very coolly and spun around to fire. But the surroundings had disappeared! I saw a person directly in front of me, who was looking at me with such love and compassion in his eyes that I was momentarily captivated by him. His eyes were steel blue and full of tears. He said nothing at all, because he didn't need to! I have never to this day felt such warmth, love, and compassion. It seemed like all eternity stopped for a brief moment.

The police report stated that I had looked like I was blinded, because I waved my gun back and forth. The police officer's partner tried to shoot me over the hood of his police car with a shotgun, but couldn't shoot because I was standing by a restaurant window, and people were in a booth eating.

I remember telling my crime partner at the trial that the black police officer testifying against us was not the person I saw! He said "Yes, it was, Steve." I never said another word to him about it. How could I?

To this day I could paint a picture of this person if I were an artist. I shall never forget it as long as I live. And today, one of my best friends is a black man. (S.M.)

S.M.'s bleak account assures us that we are never beyond the reach of God's love. What opened this man's heart to spiritual intervention? Perhaps we can see in S.M.'s desperate moment a child's pleading to be relieved of his torturous existence—and an answering response that created the possibility of a new life.

Beneath his criminal violence, we can sense S.M.'s profound fear of loving and trusting again. While his example may make us shudder, his basic fear of living is something to which all of us can relate. Most of us suffer from lesser fears that keep us from living as fully as we might. Sometimes we can trace these fears to traumatic events—such as abuse or deep emotional losses—but sometimes the sources are unknown.

L.H. developed a recurrent nightmare after finding herself living virtually alone while her husband traveled. After experiencing numerous frightful nightmares, Jesus appeared at her bedside in the middle of the night. His presence had a twofold effect: The nightmares ceased altogether, and she was never again afraid to be alone.

Since my childhood I always had a deep belief in God and Christ Jesus.

I was born in Santa Fe, New Mexico, and came to California at age sixteen. I married at eighteen. My husband is from Baghdad, Iraq. When I got to his country, I could not speak Arabic or Turkish. His family spoke both languages, plus English. My husband's business took him to different parts of the country, and I had to stay home with his family. Because of the language barrier and my being in a foreign land, I became lonely and frightened.

I started having bad nightmares, during which I felt something evil grabbing my legs, and then I would wake up. One night, toward the early morning hours, I saw Jesus sitting at the foot of my bed. I sat up and embraced him, and he put his arms around me, too. He cradled my head on his shoulder and I wept. Christ said to me, "Never be afraid because I will always be there with you." I fell asleep again. My nightmares stopped and I am never afraid to be alone

since I had my Christ encounter. It was a beautiful experi-
ence. Now I am fifty-three years old. That took place
thirty-five years ago. (L.H.)

L.H. received the reassurance she needed to deal with her fear
in that moment. More significantly, she received a promise that
Christ would always be with her. He didn't say, "only if you are
good." As we have seen in so many other accounts, his promise to
L.H. seems unconditional and eternal.

The Healing of Relationships

Interpersonal relationships are usually the source of our emotional
turmoil, so it's not surprising that many of the accounts of
emotional healing are related to this area. Many of us grow up in
such turmoil that we enter adulthood fearing that we will never find
anyone who will stand beside us. These feelings sometimes prevent
us from ever taking the necessary risks to find out if an enduring
relationship is even possible. There is simply no way to know how
we will fare on the other side of committing ourselves to another
person. In the following account, Jesus appears to a teenage girl
who was experiencing anxiety about life and her future, and
reassures her about her future marriage and family.

When I was a teenager I had an encounter with Christ.
Although I had a loving and supportive family, I had
troubled teen years. I had the habit of praying every night
before I went to sleep. One night as I was praying, the face of
Jesus became so vividly imprinted in my mind that I was
compelled to open my eyes, and sure enough, there was Jesus
in the corner of my room! But I could only see his face, and
although his lips didn't move, he told me not to worry, that I

would have a husband, one son, and one daughter. He also said that I would have a white house in town (I was living on a farm), and my husband would have a blue-collar job, and we would be very happy.

Now I know this sounds completely senseless! But I cannot begin to explain the peace and joy and sense of relief that I felt inside of me. Those feelings that night are inexpressible! When I boarded the school bus the next morning I wanted to shout that I had seen Christ! But I didn't, of course, because I would have been laughed at. I have never told anyone of my encounter. It still sounds crazy to me, but I know it happened. Without a doubt I know that.

A couple of years later I married a boy who I knew was for me from the time of our very first date. Five years later we adopted a baby girl, and two years after that we adopted a baby boy. My husband was in blue-collar work the first twenty-five years of our marriage, and his attempt at white-collar management failed miserably for very strange, unusual, and unforeseen circumstances. After much personal stress, he is back in blue-collar work and much happier. The first home we lived in was white, although when we had our children, our home was another color.

We have been married thirty-three years, and although these later years have been a little less than happy, we had an unusually happy life when our children were young.

Christ has never appeared to me again in that way, but I know now how wonderful it will feel to meet him at the end of my life on this earth. (A.R.)

As a counselor, I know that the foreknowledge Jesus conveyed to A.R. would greatly assist some of my clients, who have been so wounded by past relationships that they have become fearful, and even cynical. While it is easy to understand why Christ's appearance might not be needed by those who are still strong enough to take risks and grow through the process, we can see why his presence might be considered the "treatment of choice" when unrelenting hopelessness sets in.

Individuals who have been mistreated as children will often carry their wounds all their lives. As children, they were unable to understand that their parents had a problem, so they took the responsibility upon themselves, thinking that if they could only be better, or accept more responsibility for those around them, then the anguish would stop. Consequently, as adults, these individuals may too readily accept the familiar abusive treatment that can come from bosses, lovers, or spouses. Or, conversely, they may avoid close relationships in order to prevent the old abuse from happening again. It's at this point that a Christ encounter can have a potent, transformative influence.

A woman whose brother committed suicide when he was only twelve had always believed that she was responsible for his death. At least this is what her family had told her. Forty years later, she learned differently when Christ appeared to her while she was bathing one night.

Forty years ago, my twelve-year-old brother Jerry committed suicide. Since that time, I have been told that it was my fault, and that if I had only let him wax the new family car that final Sunday afternoon, he would still be alive. No one has ever admitted that it was a suicide. It was, according to

*my family, an accident, even though my brother hung
himself with a broken horse rein.*

*I finally went into counseling to deal with the pain and
guilt that I still felt after forty years. Then a few months
later, on September 25, 1996, I opted to take a hot bath and,
while in the tub, I read an article about Saint Dominic—
that is, as long as I could keep my glasses from fogging up.*

*I guess I listened to a subtle inner prompting, because
without thinking about it, I put the article and my glasses
down, and laid back in the tub—something I rarely do.*

*I suddenly sensed that God was present with me—just
above me and to the left, it seemed. He "spoke," but not
audibly: His thoughts just came to me. He told me that he
was going to show me why I had so much pain inside me. He
said it was because I had carried other people's pain since I
was a little girl, because I didn't think they could carry it
themselves.*

*He first showed me how I took on my brother Johnny's
pain. Johnny was two and a half years younger than I was,
but I felt I had to take care of him. Our mother and father
fought all the time. Dad would hit her, and Johnny would
cry. I would hug him and tell him that he didn't have to be
afraid. Then I would watch to see when Dad went outside, so
I could tell Johnny when he was gone. Then Mom would
come and pick Johnny up and soothe him. I didn't cry during
this, I just helped my brother. I could see myself standing in
the playpen, watching Mom hugging Johnny, while I
appeared not to be showing any emotion at all.*

*It was at this point that Jesus appeared in the place
where God had been before. He told me to hold out my hands*

and form a cup. He then placed something in my cupped hands. He said it was Johnny's and Mom's pain. There was nothing visible that I could see, but I could feel the weight. I asked him what I was supposed to do with it. He instructed me to put it anywhere I wanted to, but that I was to carry it. So I put it on my left shoulder.

He then showed me how I took on Mom's anger and pain when Dad hit her, so it wouldn't hurt her so much, and how I carried the boys' sadness as we were growing up. I even saw how I had taken on the pain of the cows that Dad used to beat so horribly. The horses, too. I seemed to put on layer after layer of pain, until I didn't think I could carry any more of it, but Jesus kept showing me more.

During this time we communicated telepathically. I finally asked him to tell me if I was responsible for Jerry's death. He said that I was not. He told me Jerry had lived as long as he did because of me. When I asked him where Jerry's pain came from, he said it came from my parents' not giving him his rightful place in the family. Even though Jerry was the youngest, Donald was the "sickly" one, so he was treated like the youngest child. Consequently, Jerry didn't think our parents wanted him. Coming eleven months after Donald, I am sure they told him—as they had told me—that he had "come too soon."

After I had taken on all of this pain, I could hardly move. I told Jesus that I just couldn't carry it all. He said I had carried this amount and more for many, many years.

Finally, he said that it was time for me to give him all of the pain. He then told me to hand some of it to him. He took it from me, and reached out for more. I kept giving it to him *until I felt like I could carry what was left, but he said that he wanted it all. I assured him that it was okay, that I could keep it. He didn't get angry, but he insisted that he wanted it all. I continued to give it to him until I had none left.*

At one point, he made a statement that I would get married again, and that I would be happy and taken care of in my old age. I told him that I didn't want to get married again. He said he understood, but that he was going to help me do it the right way. He said I would meet someone, get to know him, enjoy doing things with him, and then discover that I was in love with him. I wish Jesus had not told me that part, because I don't want to meet anyone new.

When he'd taken the last of the pain, I felt so light. I hadn't really looked at him during the vision, but I wanted to see what he was doing. I really didn't expect to see him when I looked. But he was there! He looked into my eyes and smiled. He had the most beautiful smile. It seemed so peaceful and spontaneous, and so natural and real. He just smiled at me. Nothing more, nothing less. I felt more loved and safer than I ever have before. Then he was gone, but the feeling of his peace stayed with me.

I still wonder, what did I do to deserve his coming to me in that tub of water in my nakedness—to love me just as I was. *All I can say is, Thank you, God, and thank you, Jesus.* (J.K.)

It is interesting to see how Christ makes J.K. aware of what she has done before he relieves her of her burden. He awakens her to the problem and then resolves it with his love. Most of us would just as soon skip the first part, and have Christ take our burdens from us without having to face such a thorough reenactment of our mistakes. But there would be little growth in that, and we would probably resume doing what we've always done as soon as Christ made his exit. In fact, J.K. reports awakening the next morning and, without even recalling the events of the night, praying to God to be healed of her lifelong pain. She was surprised, and then ashamed, to hear a voice tell her that she'd been healed of that problem the night before! J.K. quickly recalled the extraordinary encounter and was able to accept the healing that had transpired.

Christ appeared to another woman in a failing marriage, not to encourage her to end her marriage or to go ahead with an affair that was available to her, but to tell her simply that she was "not where he wanted her to be." Christ established his profound love for R.S., but as he often does in such life-changing encounters, he left it entirely up to her to set her own course.

It was the early 1980s and my life was in turmoil. I had two healthy children, a nice home, and a husband whom I loved, but he was a tormented Viet Nam veteran who turned to alcohol to deal with the war's insanity. He refused to admit that he was an alcoholic and would not seek treatment. I was very unhappy, but lived with the hope that my husband would come to his senses. My needs were not being met; I was an emotional wreck.

In the context of my misery, a man from my church approached me to have an affair. He stated that he had been attracted to me for some time, that he had an unhappy marriage, and that he felt that I was unhappy, too. He was charming and made me laugh. I told him that I would think about the situation and let him know of my decision in a few days.

The next morning I was at home alone as my children were in school and my husband was working. I was in the kitchen washing my hair at the sink; my head was under the running water. Suddenly, I knew *that someone was in the kitchen with me. I came up from under the faucet, water still pouring from the faucet, and water from my hair running down my clothes and on to the kitchen floor.*

I turned around and there, standing in my kitchen, was Jesus! Precious Jesus! I immediately fell to my knees and started crying uncontrollably. I said his name over and over, "Jesus, Jesus," with my head bowed. His power raised my head up and I saw his two outstretched hands. He said to me, "You are not where I want you to be."

I have never felt such love. He bathed me with his hands around my head. I felt so unworthy to be experiencing this visit. His love was so divine that I cannot find words to describe it. I felt his touch in my body, mind, and spirit; it was wonderful! I asked him to help me and to forgive me. Then I became aware that he was fading—that he was moving away from me. I cried, "Please don't go; I can do anything if you are here with me. Please don't go!"

I do not know how long the water had been pouring from the faucet or how much time had passed. I do know that the sound of the running water brought me back to the present. Water was all over the floor and my clothes were soaked. I felt exhausted, and I was in awe of what I had experienced. I also felt sad that he had gone.

At that time I interpreted Jesus' words to be a message not to engage in the affair, and so I did not. I came to learn, however, that his words had an even deeper meaning.

I began to face the reality that I could not live with the alcoholism anymore. I began counseling with my minister and started attending Al-Anon, a twelve-step self-help program for families of alcoholics. I got the courage to divorce my husband and got my kids and myself into counseling with a great therapist who was just the person we needed. Several years later, I reentered college after a twenty-year absence. I started acknowledging the intuitive gifts that I had been aware of even as a child. I majored in psychology and planned to work in mental health.

But God had another plan. Today, I am a program director in an outpatient program for substance abuse! I encounter many Viet Nam veterans. I have just returned to college again to pursue either a special study in substance abuse or a master's degree.

I know without a doubt that Jesus' words totally changed my life and are still changing my life. They gave me the courage to change my direction. *And his visit was so precious that I still find it difficult to describe. I repeat, I have never experienced such love. Unworthy as I feel, I know that God has a mission for me, that he saw something in me that I couldn't see in myself, and that he honored me with a visit from his Son.*

In so many ways, I feel that I have only just begun. (R.S.)

R.S. took a variety of steps on the basis of her visitation from Jesus. Out of a willingness to change the direction of her life, she activated a fuller capacity to serve others. It is interesting, once again, that Jesus did not specify what changes needed to take place: He essentially entrusted her with the task of setting her own course.

But his dramatic interventions left no doubt that urgent changes were necessary.

K.S. was twenty-two and in a troubled relationship when she had her Christ encounter. It gave her the reassurance she needed eventually to end a destructive relationship.

I had been involved with a man for most of my teen and adult years, and the relationship had not been a healthy one for me or for him. Over the years, we had grown apart. I was looking for the answer to how or if I should end the relationship. One day, my boyfriend and I went bow hunting deep in the woods. I was not hunting—I merely wanted to be with him and to enjoy nature. My boyfriend brought me to a hunting blind made of rocks and told me to stay there until he came back, for my own safety.

I had little with me to entertain myself—just a backpack with some food and apple juice. So I engrossed myself in a study of nature. I really looked at the colors of the leaves, the insects crawling near me, and the glorious blue sky.

At one point, I was meditating on the troubles of my relationship. I looked up at the sun, partially hidden behind leaves, and it seemed to pulsate. I saw a face in the sun that resembled Christ. Being cautious, when I heard a voice speak to me, I asked, "Who are you?" The light vision pulsated and answered, "Some call me Buddha, some call me Christ." I said, "I don't know Buddha." And he answered, "Then I am Christ." I looked over at my boyfriend who was passing by and I felt love for him, but felt detached from him. I don't recall most of my conversation with Christ, but I know I spoke of my fear of leaving my boyfriend, of "failing" my boyfriend, of being alone if I left him. The one phrase that I remember distinctly is Christ saying, "I am with you always."

That phrase, that voice, that face has been a great source of comfort to me in the years since then. I have finally freed myself from that unhealthy relationship. As of yet, I have not found a new love, but I am confident that he is out there.

And that he is out there to be with me always as he promised his apostles. (K.S.)

Christ doesn't say to K.S., "You don't need men, only me." He lets her know that whatever happens, his love will not abandon her. Obviously, he offers a different kind of relationship in which K.S. can find the security often lacking in ordinary human relationships.

The being's answer to K.S.'s question, "Who are you?" underscores our difficulty in conclusively identifying the being who appears in some of these encounters. The being does not say that he is Christ or Buddha—he implies that he is both at the same time. It is certainly difficult to comprehend how this can be. But rather than rejecting the validity of this experience because it puzzles, or offends us, we might do well to consider—as an exercise in humility—that God is so great and mysterious that he is willing to be known by other names.

In an account similar in effect to K.S.'s, a thirty-two-year-old woman was feeling the loneliness that comes from knowing that an emotional relationship is over. Again, Christ manifested to remind C.A.M. of his enduring love for her.

I was at a very low point at the end of an intense personal relationship. My male friend was throwing a "welcome to spring" party one Friday night, and I knew it would be too wild for my frame of mind. I therefore made arrangements to stay at a hotel for the night.

I settled in for the evening, complete with book, food, and TV. As I compared the differences in my emotions now as to when I first met this person, the most glaring awareness was, "I'm alone again. I'm alone again and I've accomplished nothing. Here I am, right back where I started. Has all that I've gone through here been for nothing?" As I sadly thought this, the room changed subtly. A feeling of utter peace descended, and to the left where the balcony and sliding glass doors were located, the area brightened. I felt a presence fill that area and a feeling of being absolutely loved swept over me and filled me. I knew it was Jesus. I mentally heard a voice say, "You are not alone. You have me." We communicated, then the presence withdrew, back out the doors where he had first entered. I was renewed. I should add that the significance of the balcony is that beyond it lies the ocean which held a lot of meaning for me.

Rough circumstances followed, but I'm still holding on to the faith this experience instilled within me. From that night on, I feel that the course of my life was redirected, reshaped. I discovered an inner strength that was lacking before I heard the simple declaration, "You are not alone." (C.A.M.)

Besides providing the emotional support individuals usually need before terminating a destructive relationship, Christ's intervention can also apparently improve a relationship by removing some of the obstacles which stand in the way of deeper trust and intimacy. In the following account, the witness experiences relief in two areas, one of them directly related to her marriage.

I joined a charismatic prayer group at a time when I was open to my spiritual life. I was in a state of excitement and grace while at the same time aware of a spirit of fear.

I felt this fear at night when I would walk from my room toward my newborn daughter's room down the hall at night to nurse her. It was a fear of the dark and an "evil" presence.

I was also in the process of deep contemplative and persistent prayer requesting God for a healing that would positively affect my sexual relationship with my husband.

One morning between 4:00 and 6:00 A.M., I "awoke" to a feeling that penetrated my very being with a warmth and a joy that was overwhelming. I opened my eyes and saw Jesus "hovering" or floating before and above me as I lay in my bed. His arms were stretched out and opened—as if welcoming me or blessing me.

I recall vividly the love in his face. I felt I was looking at his face with my soul. His face and upper body were visible and translucent, but his body was covered in a flowing robe.

Love was radiating from his face into my body and I felt it physically as warmth and glowing and throbbing vibrations. The best way to explain it in human terms would be a spiritual-sexual experience.

Since then, my fear of the dark has lessened and I have come to realize that I am capable of experiencing orgasm. I do not know if there is any connection between my experience of Jesus and my prayers in this regard. (2nd M.M.)

M.M.'s encounter with Jesus apparently healed her on at least two levels, and yet not a word was spoken. The impact of his love was, once again, completely sufficient to activate the healing process.

Our sexuality is a particularly sensitive area of our lives, and to imagine anyone intervening specifically at that level can easily awaken a sense of discomfort or embarrassment. And yet, as we have seen, Christ's presence has a global rather than an isolated effect—he expresses his love for us as complete persons, and then the impact of such complete regard reaches into any area where healing is needed. From this standpoint, M.M.'s sexual feelings during the encounter merely indicated where healing was taking place.

Sometimes when we adopt new, higher ideals, or affirm a closer, more committed relationship with God, our lives take a turn for the worse before they get better. All of our unfinished business from the past comes back to haunt us—our regrettable choices, our hurtful actions, and our unresolved pain from old relationships. We find ourselves looking in the mirror at a person who has failed time and time again to respond to a higher calling. And the awareness that we have fallen so short can be enough to make us conclude that we are hopeless. We become depressed because we have awakened to our "fallen state."

J.M.S. experienced Christ coming to her following her slide into a depression that came over her after embarking on what she thought would be an exciting, uplifting spiritual journey.

I began to meditate and pray, attempting to draw the light of Christ from within myself. In meditation I found warmth and peace of mind, harmony and relaxation. Out of meditation, however, I found myself introspecting and analyzing different areas of my present life with criticism and negativity. The "snowballing" effect of those few weeks of intense introspection consumed me with depression, doubt, fear, and anxiety. Worst of all, I found myself feeling unworthy of the Father's love.

In the midst of this suffering and burdensome consciousness, Jesus came to me in a concise and vivid dream. I stood in a narrow white hallway with a doorway at the end. Jesus stood in the doorway dressed in a simple long white robe, without sash or embellishment. Behind Jesus was a grayness or gray cloud. The very second my eyes met his, he turned. The symbolic movement meant everything to me! The impression I immediately received was, "Follow me and have faith." The grayness disturbed me, for I expected a path paved with gold. But my path with Jesus has its crosses. I believe he appeared to me so I would find strength in him and carry on.

My perception of everything following the dream has taken on a new light in the grayness. My love and spiritual awareness of Our Lord only deepens with time. (J.M.S.)

As we have seen in so many of the Christ encounters, his appearance signaled a new beginning for J.M.S., even though the path ahead looked somber in its grayness. With his silent gesture, he does not deny the bleakness of her life, but instead calls her to follow him into it, and through it.

Some Christ encounter recipients have reported feeling so loved by Christ after their experience that they were able to weather lengthy ordeals with surprising ease and confidence. One woman had experienced massive rejection. Not only had her church rejected her, but her husband had apparently lost all respect and love for her; and the kids had picked up his attitude and begun to verbally abuse her. It was hard to imagine a way out of this abysmal situation.

Some of the darkest times I've faced began with my excommunication from a Christian fellowship due to a misunderstanding, and culminated nine years later when I developed a brain tumor that had to be removed.

During that "dark night of the soul," I had one more experience which to me was the most profoundly beautiful experience of my entire life. I remember it clearly because it happened on Valentine's Day.

My husband came to bed well after midnight as is customary. But he proceeded to wake me up to fuss at me about the way I wasn't keeping the house clean. I had a broken ankle and had been scooting around on my fanny, cast and all, to pick up after the children, who should have been doing it themselves.

I'm not a naturally organized or tidy person, and I have to exert real effort to maintain a semblance of order. But the children, after seeing their father's disrespect of me, were being particularly rude to me during that time. Still, I was blamed for their behavior because I "allowed it." I was frustrated and at a low point emotionally because I was physically incapacitated and the situation was totally out of control.

My husband chose that night to tell me that he no longer loved me and that he felt he and the children would be better off without me. I remember asking him if he was willing to try and work things out, and he said, "No."

I got out of bed and hobbled to the living room on my crutches and sank down into the couch. I know that I cried for several hours until I was totally spent. I told Jesus that my children and husband didn't love me and treated me with great dishonor. I told him that I had no one left but him.

At that moment, I felt the sofa cushion beside me sink down and felt someone sit down beside me. I reached my hand over hoping it might possibly be my husband, but there was no one there physically. Then I felt a warm and loving arm go around my shoulder, and was suddenly immersed in the most unconditional love imaginable. I knew that no matter what happened to me, he was enough. It was as if I became a totally detached party in the whole situation with my family.

The sense of love and total peace lasted for more than six months without being broken by any situation or person. I knew that I could lose everything physically, but still have everything that mattered—because I had Jesus, and that nothing and no one could ever separate me from his love.

Since that time, in all fairness, I must say that God has been allowed to work out his love in our home and marriage. But there are still times when I yearn for that total completeness I felt when, for a season, he protected me and he was all I had. (2nd B.S.)

I grew up in the same small town with this woman, and we went through school together from first grade to graduation. She was the kind of person that other kids sometimes make fun of: She was too nice and old-fashioned to fit easily into the crowd. As an adult, I have come to see her with new eyes—as one of those special people endowed with a sweetness and innocence that is too easily taken for granted and ridiculed by the world. It was easy to understand why a person like her would be open to Christ's presence. Indeed, this experience was her fourth. One might think that this experience would finally resolve her unusual hardships. But this is not always the way it works, it seems. When I last spoke to her, she was battling cancer again, even though her relationships with her family have become more loving and fulfilling.

B.S.'s sustained ordeal calls to mind the lives of well-known Christian mystics—like John of the Cross and Teresa of Avila—who underwent periods of extreme hardship, illness, despair, or depression. Sophisticated Christian thinkers have come to see this "dark night of the soul" as a necessary testing stage in the spiritual journey, rather than an embarrassing footnote in the lives of otherwise devout individuals. It is a period in which the seeker comes face-to-face with his unresolved fears and attachments, and is called upon to muster a new response in the face of adversity.

In her exhaustive research on Christian mysticism, Evelyn Underhill[20] observes that the dark night of the soul typically begins *not before but after* the saint's initial illumination. It is as if the bright promise of the initial awakening brings a person's less lofty characteristics into stark relief. The need to understand and integrate the less-than-exalted side of oneself may account for why the Christ encounter does not always eliminate one's struggle in an instance. It may even be that it is the *quality of the struggle*—not its complete resolution—that prepares a person for a fuller partnership with him.

> *"They who have my commandments and keep them are*
> *those who love me; and those who love me will be loved by*
> *my Father, and I will love them and reveal myself to them."*
> John 14:21

5

Confrontation

"I have come to show you what you have built."
G.S.S.

WHEN JESUS TOLD PETER THAT HE WOULD DENY HIS
Master three times before morning came, his disciple was understandably upset and intent on proving Jesus wrong. But when the
opportunities arose in which Peter could have affirmed his
devotion to Jesus, he denied knowing him each time. Obviously,
Jesus knew his disciple better than Peter knew himself. Why did
Jesus predict Peter's failure if he knew all along that Peter would
deny him? Perhaps because he knew that Peter's fear would
continue to threaten his commitment to those he loved—and that
by pointing out the problem, Peter would remain thereafter challenged to overcome it.

Throughout the gospel record, we find that Jesus continually
labored to awaken his disciples and followers—and even his

enemies—to what they had placed above their relationship with God. He obviously wanted them to develop beyond their limited understanding and capabilities; and he was willing to challenge them to face the obstacles standing in their way of expressing a deeper love. In this confrontational role, Jesus often orchestrated what might be appropriately called *initiations*, experiences designed to test people, and to elicit a new, deeper response from them. Not surprisingly, many of the Christ encounters included herein echo this theme of confrontation and initiation. They reveal a Christ figure bringing unfinished business to light so that the witness can eventually resolve it and come into a closer relationship with him.

Jesus himself faced numerous tests just before and during his public ministry. In the desert, he was tempted to wield the phenomenal power he could have enjoyed, but he turned it down. Later, he had to confront repeatedly the ignorance and betrayal of his followers and friends: Even when he needed their companionship the most in the Garden of Gethsemane, they could not stay awake, and he had to face the dread of his ultimate destiny alone. And finally, when he was given an opportunity to save himself by denying he was the Son of God, he said nothing to dispel this claim, and he was killed for it. Clearly, Jesus remains for us the highest example of an *initiate*: He faced and surpassed the most difficult tests imaginable, remaining devoted in an uncompromising way to his calling.

Few among us would welcome the kinds of tests Jesus himself faced. But individuals who have sought a closer relationship with God sometimes welcome the opportunity to find out whatever stands in the way of this ultimate relationship.

In some of these reports, which I have termed "confrontational" Christ encounters, the process of initiation begins, but remains incomplete. In these accounts, the witnesses encounter a situation that brings to light an unresolved problem, but they do nothing about it during the experience. They are left feeling that they have been "weighed on the scales and found wanting" (Daniel 5:27).

The Christ figure may appear rather stern as he lovingly confronts the witnesses with unresolved problems. The emotional effects of this confrontation can be quite unsettling. Even so, the confrontation points promisingly to a closer relationship if the witnesses can remove the self-imposed barriers between themselves and Christ.

In other reports, which I have termed "initiation" Christ encounters, the recipients are able to take the process further. Instead of reacting in an unthinking or habitual way to the problem being presented, they are able to respond appropriately to it during the encounter and resolve the problem before the experience ends. Once this corrective response is made, the experience typically culminates in a full encounter with Christ.

Confrontational and initiation Christ encounters are the same, except for how they end. As they unfold, they exhibit the same apparent twofold purpose: *to awaken the recipient to an unresolved problem,* and *to elicit a new response that resolves the problem.*

For some reason, some people are up for the challenge, while others are not. It might be useful in the future to examine the differences between those individuals who succeed and those who fail in meeting the tests presented. We might find, for example, that those who succeed engage in regular prayer or meditation, as a way to foster surrender to God's will. Or we might discover that they are involved in intense interpersonal relationships where they can receive regular, honest feedback concerning their own unresolved issues. Knowing what makes the difference could help us take some steps to increase the likelihood that we will respond appropriately, if and when such challenges arise.

Confrontational Christ Encounters

Many of us, if given the opportunity, would gladly meet Christ face to face. But if the following account is any indication of what we might encounter, some of us would be unable to remain in his presence—not so much by his judgment, but by our own lack of readiness for such a relationship.

I write concerning a "confrontation" with Christ that began with a dream.

I awoke shortly after 1:00 A.M., and sat bolt upright, crying, "No! God, No!" as I seemed to be forcibly thrust from Christ's presence. A powerful, unforgettable stream of love came from him as I left his presence. I then recalled the entire scene:

I was facing a figure, whom I recognized as my own "higher self" from an earlier encounter. This being was front and center and to the left of Christ.

Christ, who was not visible to me, but appeared as a formless dark shadow, asked, "Is this one ready?"

The higher self replied, "No, he is not."

Christ then asked, "Does he have 'mono-clear-eyed' vision?"

Then I answered, "I know what it is, but have not been practicing." Then I felt banished from their presence.

Again, twenty-eight years later, I awoke hearing a clear, gentle, authoritative voice asking, "Are you ready?"

Having singleness of purpose has been an elusive pursuit. My attention span is like a child's. My intentions

are solid, but sometimes I do not persevere diligently.
However, I still feel the force of the love he bestowed on me
even as I left his presence. This memory serves to bring me
back to a more focused practice of prayer, meditation,
patience, and service.

Except for that beam of love, the encounter was a devas-
tating experience that left me in shock for some time
afterward. And to some degree, I still am. (W.A.)

W.A.'s failure resembles the experiences of the knights whose adventures are described in the medieval legends of the Holy Grail. Their lifelong dream was to have a vision of the Holy Grail—the cup that Jesus used for the Last Supper with his disciples.

But after surmounting every sort of difficulty and finding their way into the Castle of the King Fisherman—the place where the Holy Grail resided—only one of the knights managed to pass a final initiation test. Only Parcifal, who witnessed the Grail paraded before him in all of its radiant splendor, had the presence of mind and heart to ask a simple question—about *whom the grail served.* Rather than becoming merely entranced by the beauty of the Grail, Parcifal asked a question that signified his own commitment to *serve whom the Grail served.* He thus passed the initiation by offering himself as one who would fulfill the Grail's purpose. By remaining so singularly devoted, Parcifal ushered in a glorious new era, when the waters flowed again upon the wasteland, and the Fisher King, who could not heal his own painful wound, was finally healed.

Parcifal did not succeed all at once. The story tells us that he managed to enter the Grail castle once before as a young man, but failed to ask the crucial question. Only after years of heroic effort and maturation did Parcifal manage to witness the Grail for the second time. Like W.A., Parcifal was unprepared for the initial encounter; but he was able to learn from his failure, and eventually become conscious of the "clear-eyed" response that was required of him. We see in the Grail myth a hopeful two-step initiation motif of *initial failure borne of ignorance* giving way to eventual *success based on a mature conscious understanding* of the singular aim of the initiation process—giving oneself fully in service to a higher calling.

W.A. felt banished when he realized that he had neglected doing what was required of him to be in deeper communion with Christ. Similarly, the following confrontational encounter—which is one of my own—was apparently arrested by my hasty flight from the frightening dream scenario. I, too, realized that I did not have what it took to deal with a frightening test. In this Christ encounter, Jesus exhibits an attitude that is both loving and stern as he assumes a highly confrontational stance toward me. I had this experience in my late twenties, and it left me sobered by its implications.

I dreamed that I was returning from a long journey. I knew that I had been wayward and indulgent during the time away. I carried a large, ornate, silver cross studded with gems. I supported it against my side, much like a Catholic priest might carry a cross during a procession.

I walked down a dusty street of a primitive village and turned the corner only to see Jesus standing with a group of men. They all faced me with stern expressions. Jesus said with love and firmness, "I have come to show you what you have built. The only reason I do so is because your Father wants me to, and because I do this so well." As I stood puzzled by this, he hurled a flame-tipped lance toward me. Passing through my sleeve, but missing my flesh, it impaled my arm against a stucco wall behind me. Then he threw another one, which anchored my other arm.

Immediately, I found myself in another place—in a battle or in a gladiator's arena. A large, powerful man in a cloth headdress stood over me. He proceeded to tell me with malicious pleasure how he was going to kill me. Realizing that I must have been dreaming, I forced myself awake. (G.S.S.)

Years after this dream, I discovered that the lance was highly regarded in the Grail myths. Actually, it was so important that the vision of the Grail was believed in many accounts to include a vision of a lance hovering above it. Dripping Christ's blood into the Grail, the lance was thought to be the weapon which pierced Christ's side once he had died on the cross. And it was also the weapon that wounded the Fisher King. Why would such a violent image occupy such a sacred place in these myths?

Robert Johnson[21] points out that the lance had come to symbolize to the medieval mind the incisive, discriminating wisdom that we need to get to the heart of what matters most: After all, it was what released Christ's essence for the benefit of all humanity. As such, says Johnson, the lance is symbolic of the highest expression of masculinity. A measure of the respect afforded the lance survives today in the Greek Orthodox communion Mass, where the host is broken by a small lance.

In one of the Grail stories, Sir Gawain says to King Arthur, "We have won everything by the lance and lost everything by the sword." Referring to the sword as the primitive, destructive aspect of the male psyche, Gawain's words allude, in my own dream, to the gladiator who appeared before me in the arena. Wielding brute power, he was the opposite of Jesus, who wielded power through the lance—incisively and without any real harm. *In essence, the lance symbolizes Christ's stance in every confrontational encounter. It is an attitude which is at once wounding—in that he awakens us painfully to our unresolved dilemmas—and healing, in that his love sustains us in resolving whatever remains before us on our journey.*

I came to realize that the warrior in my dream represented, on one hand, my own formidable, aggressive, and destructive tendencies. I also realized that he symbolized aggressive individuals who would awaken in me a sense of powerlessness—the flip side of the problem. With this realization, I came to see that I could resolve this dilemma, not by further suppressing my aggression or by lashing out in anger, but by claiming and using the lance—that is, by using my assertiveness in a conscious, constructive way, and by accepting the challenge of dealing fearlessly with aggressive, critical individuals.

The following account has elements of both a confrontational and an initiation encounter. During the first part of the dream, the dreamer—a forty-nine-year-old art dealer who was in his late twenties at the time—succeeds in overcoming his fear sufficiently to come face-to-face with a being who, at first, reveals itself as a great whale. But later, Christ himself confronts the dreamer with a problem that cannot be resolved in the course of the dream.

I dreamed that I was on a journey with a group of fellow seekers. There were twelve of us. I recognized several of them as friends and acquaintances. They were all seekers. Some were mature, some less so. A few seemed advanced and sort of quiet. Others were a bit more naive and boisterous. There was a sense of excitement and anticipation among them concerning the adventures that we were to undergo on our journey.

We were riding barrels, each of us straddling a floating barrel as we proceeded along a rocky shoreline with cliffs to the left of us and a vast sea to our right. We sort of hugged the shoreline as it was important to maintain our balance on the floating barrel so we didn't tip over and fall in, and get dashed in the rocks.

I was riding the last barrel in the lineup, and my friend and mentor Herb was the "leader" of the group. He and I were intentionally at the rear of the line so as to watch over and assist anyone who might have an accident or get into trouble.

Suddenly, there was great commotion and shouting from the others. As they pointed out to sea, two great whales appeared far out on the horizon. There was a sense of excitement and fear, for they could easily swamp us. I was apprehensive and yet I wished, how I wished from the deepest yearnings of my heart, that I could meet what surely must be God's greatest creation—the Great Whale.

Before I completed the thought, the whales knew of my desire and began rushing into shore at a tremendous speed. One stopped and waited, while the other one continued straight toward me. My feelings were mixed. I was terrified and elated at the same time. I tried to remain brave and calm. I was determined not to try to escape, but to face it head-on. Swamped or not, I wished to meet the whale.

At the last second before impact, the whale stopped. Raising its massive head out of the water, it bowed its head before me and softly brushed my right knee. The contact felt sacred. I felt its respect for me, and for who I was. I felt deeply, deeply honored. I felt that the encounter is a great gift.

As it swam back out to the companion whale, it turned back, emerging halfway out of the water and transforming itself into a very dapper Jewish male in his mid-thirties who is wearing a dark blue three-piece suit. The other whale transformed itself similarly. The first man invited us to dinner at his home, high up on the cliff.

The home was beautiful, like a castle. A feast was being prepared outside on the cliff top, and it was a beautiful, sunny day. Herb began introducing us to our host, who turned out to be Jesus! In a quiet and shy manner, I hung back, feeling that the others should go first. I just hoped there would be enough time for me to meet him, too, though I was willing to forgo the opportunity if need be. I wondered why it seemed easy for the others, and I wished I could feel more a part of the group.

Herb finally gestured toward me, and said to Jesus, "And now I want you to meet M.R. He has worked diligently to serve you and your cause." I was overwhelmed at Herb's introduction.

At this point, Jesus turned and looked at me. He was beautiful. He gazed at me and his eyes penetrated to the depths of my being. He knew everything about me. He knew me like I have never been known before. His look stilled me; and I was not elated nor ashamed. I just felt known—absolutely and utterly known.

I knew that just by looking into my eyes, he could tell that what Herb said was true. He raised his index finger to me and said:

"I can see that what you say is true. But you have one problem, and that is you are too romantic. And that makes for confusing considerations."

At this point, I burst into tears. I did not feel in the least bit reprimanded, only incredible love from him and for him. I felt thankful beyond measure.

It has been almost twenty years since I had this dream. In rewriting it, it has just as much impact on me now as it did back then. I can only love this Jesus with my entire being, my whole heart and soul. I feel willing to serve him forever.
(M.R.)

Once M.R. actually encounters Jesus, his experience resembles that of a life review, which is a widely reported feature of many near-death experiences. When Jesus looks into M.R.'s eyes, he feels totally known and exposed by Jesus' gaze—yet totally accepted, too. Jesus expresses the same unparalleled, discriminating awareness that was symbolized by the lance in my own encounter with him: It's what he does "so well."

In M.R.'s case, however, we find that the pain of discovering the unresolved problem is more than offset by the immense love and self-acceptance he experienced in that singular life-changing moment.

M.R. seems ready for the life review, while others have found this scrutiny much more difficult to bear. For instance, Dannion Brinkley—who had a near-death experience when he was struck by lightning—was brought before a Being of Light who was accompanied by twelve attendant beings. Together, they ushered him through a review of his life. Brinkley says that he was totally unprepared for the emotional pain of witnessing his own life in review.

But years later, when he had a second near-death experience, the work he had done in the meantime—specifically, his efforts to *love* others—made the life review much more tolerable. Brinkley's message to others is to *work on loving those you have not loved*; for that, he says, is the *only* criterion by which he felt evaluated in the presence of the Being of Light.[22]

If the problems brought to light by the confrontational encounter are important enough to warrant Christ's involvement, then our response to them probably exerts a significant impact on our lives. In some instances, our responses could feasibly be a life-or-death matter. For example, one of my own confrontational Christ encounters hinted strongly that my very life depended on a willingness to do what I was "called to do." Without actually telling me that I might die, Christ seems to point out the inevitable—that avoiding my own path might unwittingly undermine my reason for living.

I mentioned this account in the Introduction, but it bears repeating in more detail because it demonstrates just how our response to a confrontational Christ encounter can be a life-and-death matter.

I am with my friend Mark and we are both aware that we are dreaming. We begin flying crisscross patterns through a large new auditorium, as if we are preparing it and consecrating it. We actually interpenetrate each other as we simultaneously pass through the center of the room.

At one point I see him standing in a doorway at the back of the auditorium, talking to someone standing behind the door. I know it is Jesus! Anxiously, I walk through the door and look toward him. At first I am only able to see a bright

*white light. But then the light abruptly changes into the clear
form of the Master.*

*He looks just as I would expect Jesus to appear, except
his hair and beard seem quite dark, and his features sharper.
He seems stern, but I feel his love for me. As I stand there,
saying nothing, awed by his presence, he asks, "Are you ready
to leave the earth yet?" Startled by the implications of his
question, I say, "No." Then he says, "Then go out and do
what you know to do." (G.S.S.)*

Jesus did not have to tell me that I was ambivalent in my
commitment. His question left no doubt of that. At the time, I was
considering abandoning some of the goals regarding spiritual work
that I had pursued up to that point. And yet his attitude was so
loving that I could feel that there was actually no judgment coming
from him. Instead there was only a loving intent to point out my
apparently precarious hold on life due to my failure to heed my own
deeper calling to serve him.

I did not say, "Of course I will do it." It took me a long while to
come around to that. And yet in a couple of confrontational Christ
encounters, the witnesses responded to Christ's initial confrontation with a "corrective response" within hours or days of the
encounter. By so doing, these witnesses essentially converted a
confrontational Christ encounter into an experience of full
initiation.

For instance, one twelve-year-old girl had a remarkable pair of
experiences that demonstrated the impact of a corrective response.
In the first she was confronted with God's wrath. Then, chastened
by the overwhelming experience, she remained in a prayerful state
for several days afterward and took symbolic measures to cleanse

herself. This response then seemed to pave the way for a harmonious culmination in a subsequent Christ encounter. Writing in midlife about these events, she reports:

> *When I was around twelve years old, I decided to tease my sister Dorothy. I piled dirt clods on top of our outdoor toilet and waited for her to go use it. As she emerged, I dropped clods on her. Trying to elude the clods, she finally broke and ran for the house. I jumped off the toilet and reared back to throw another clod at Dorothy. She ran to the left to escape me. Just as I was about to let go and hit her, I heard a voice. (While it took only two seconds for this to happen, it takes a while to explain the voice and my experience which ensued.)*
>
> *The voice sounded like thunder passing through water— like waves. All the voice actually said was, "Drop that." These words were Spirit as they entered me; and they were pure wrath. They washed through me from the top of my head out the soles of my feet. I immediately began to try to open my hand and found I couldn't do it. I struggled several times to open my fingers and couldn't. I felt destruction all around me and realized I could be destroyed on the spot. I recognized this voice as God.*
>
> *Because I trusted God . . . I found myself trusting him regardless of whether I lived or died. As I submitted to him, I felt his words turn to pure mercy. This washed over me again from top to bottom. The mercy seemed to enter my heart like a trickle first. Then like a dam breaking, his mercy flooded my heart and being. Then, his words turned to pure love. This washed over me the same as before. This mercy and love seemed to run together with the mercy and love I knew, and*

we were one in Spirit. I felt like I came through it only because I submitted and only because of the mercy of God.

When I submitted and quit trying to open my hand, all of a sudden I felt like a puppet. My hand opened by his power and the rock fell out. I turned around to see where the voice came from. It had come from the north. I looked and saw nothing. I felt this great sense of redemption, like I'd been purchased at a great price. I then heard Mom calling me.

Later . . .I dreamed that my feet were dirty and I was outside. I heard my phone ringing and I went to answer it. When I did I found myself at a dinner. There were white tables and plates. I sat down and ate two bites (which I believe to mean the two words God spoke to me). Then I asked to help serve and was told, "Yes, but why are you dressed that way? You have to go and change." Then I returned and served the table. I awoke and thought that was an odd dream.

For guidance on the dream, I opened my Bible and it fell to the guest who came to dinner. I then felt a strong urge to wash my feet. They appeared clean, but nonetheless I washed them in a pan of water.

I felt very prayerful for the next four days. I went to bed early one night to pray. Just as my head touched the pillow, I saw clouds in front of my eyes, and an opening came in the clouds. I saw myself standing before an altar with a wooden cross behind it. I closed my eyes thinking this would go away, but then I saw a "man of light" who looked like sunlight. He was in the form of a man. I called him Shiolah, as if I knew him. I also heard a still, quiet voice say, "The Christ."

I then saw a lamb work its way from my heart and run to him. He stood there with his arms outstretched; and this lamb (who I knew was me) leapt into his arms. He petted and stroked the lamb. The vision went away and then came back. Then the man of light stood by a sheepfold. He set the lamb into a fold at his right side, by his feet. They were in a green pasture and all ate in his light. He was the only light— all else was darkness. The lamb who was me ate of the green pasture. The man of light stooped to pet the lamb. He straightened and looked at me, there on the bed, and wrath came into his face. Then it left and he held out his arms to me again. (D.B.)

Taken together, D.B.'s experiences run the whole gamut from thoughtless act, to confrontation, to corrective response—and, finally, to a sense of Christ's forgiveness and profound love for her. Through Christ encounters like hers, we can see a single process operating in both confrontational and initiation Christ encounters. It is a process in which the witness first becomes starkly aware of what stands in the way of a closer relationship with him. Even though the potential initiate may lack the presence of mind to respond immediately and appropriately to the test when it is presented, he or she is often left knowing what needs to be done to resolve the impasse. And by taking corrective action, we can become an initiate in the highest sense of the word—willing to confront and resolve whatever stands in the way of our relationship with him.

"Those who love me will keep my word,
and my Father will love them, and we will come to them
and make our home with them."
John 14:23

6

Initiation

"Are you really ready to follow Me?"
2nd M.M.

IN CONTRAST TO CONFRONTATIONAL CHRIST encounters, the initiation encounter does not end with the witness's inability or unwillingness to resolve the problem that is presented. For reasons that we cannot fully understand, the recipients of these experiences are able to respond *during the experience* in such a way as to remove what stands in the way of a closer relationship with Christ.

Take, for instance, the story of Debra, a teenage girl who, along with her fellow cheerleaders, had been accused of drinking spiked punch at a football game. The principal of the small-town high school summoned them all on Monday morning, and proceeded to ask them one by one if they had drunk alcohol at the game. Debra was the last one in line to be asked, and she fully intended to do what the others had done: lie and escape the punishment and humiliation that would surely ensue. However, when the principal at last came to her and asked her the pointed question, she looked into his eyes and saw his entire face change into the face of Jesus. The Master looked upon her silently, but it was clear to her what she had to do: She admitted the truth without further hesitation. Although she was temporarily expelled from school, and became the talk of the town, Debra said that she remained completely at peace during the whole ordeal. Obviously, she had passed an important spiritual test, and was sustained by the inner rewards of doing the right thing.

This young woman faced a reasonable spiritual test, and her honesty provided an example in her community that served everyone's long-term interests. However, from the outside, some Christ encounter initiation tests can seem unreasonable. For instance, the recipient of the following Christ encounter—a seventy-six-year old retired nurse who was sixty-one at the time was cleaning her home one day, and heard a distinct voice asking her if she would consider doing a most difficult thing. Clearly, she underwent a most severe test of her faith.

It was a beautiful sunny January morning and I had just finished the household chores in the bedroom. As I started to go into the hallway, I heard a clear, definite voice speak to me. The voice said, "Are you really ready to follow me?" Without question I thought, I thought I had been following you all of my life. *Then the voice said, "If I ask you to leave your husband, children, and everything you know, would you do so?" I was literally stunned at the question he had asked. Without a shadow of a doubt I was sure it was Jesus who asked the question. So for the next six weeks I prepared myself, my adult children, and my husband for my departure. It wasn't that I loved any of them less; but if I were called, I had to follow him. I described to my loved ones as well as I could what had happened. It felt very final.*

When I was finally ready, I was in the same place in the house where I had heard the voice the first time. I said, "Yes, I am ready to follow." Instantly, I knew I would not have to leave my family. It was the Abraham and Isaac story all over again.

Then the voice said, "Get back in the church; you cannot change it from without." Immediately afterward, I sent to northern California for my church membership, and eventually became an elder in the church.

The second thing the voice asked me to do was to make amends with my sister. She and I had never gotten along. So I began writing her letters, many of which I tore up, but that was the process of getting my anger out in private. Eventually, she joined a group I was attending.

The third and final thing the voice said was, "Find Paula and get to know her." Paula was the daughter of my brother who had been killed in the Air Force. She was born two weeks after he was killed. I wrote her a very long letter and made a trip to see her. We stayed up many nights going through old family pictures.

Years later, when I was president of the American Holistic Health Association, I had a very difficult time with several of the board members. I had another vision. I can still see it. It was of Jesus coming down toward me from a small hill with the disciples in the background. He held out

his arms with his hands put together and said, "Put it in my
hands." I did, and things became better.
I feel he is with me at all times now. (2nd M.M.)

We can see from M.M.'s experience that the Christ encounter
can be so compelling that recipients, in their willingness to follow
Christ's guidance, may choose to ignore the wishes and opinions of
their family and friends. For those of us on the "outside," who
might stand to lose whatever influence we have previously enjoyed
in the person's life, such a turnabout might appear foolish and
destructive. And from the standpoint of a potential recipient, we
can just as easily fear the consequences of such an encounter. What
will Christ ask us to give up? What will he ask us to do that we've
always been afraid to do?

M.M.'s experience, which can be seen as both an initiation and
instructional encounter, suggests that the instructions issued by the
Christ figure during an encounter can themselves represent an initiation test. In M.M.'s case, he challenges her to confront and resolve
three neglected aspects of her religious and interpersonal life. Such
guidance contrasts with the kind of comforting advice that one
commonly seeks from other sources of guidance—yes or no
answers to already defined questions. Thus, we can reasonably
conclude that there is an intelligence operating in such Christ
encounters whose agenda differs from what the recipients might
choose consciously for themselves.

Significantly, Christ did not tell M.M. that she had to leave her
family, he *asked* her if she *would*. In many of the Christ encounters,
we find Christ awakening and stimulating the recipients through
probing, revealing questions. As we know from the gospel record,
Jesus frequently asked questions as a way to elicit a deeper response

from those around him—as if their search into their memories and into their own consciences would stir to life some untapped realization.

In two different Christ encounters—one in a dream and another while meditating—Christ "merely" asked me questions that resulted in a sense of discovery about myself and deeper truths that I had not acknowledged. Both felt like initiations, however, because the particular answers I arrived at seemed crucial to the furthering of our relationship.

The first encounter happened while I was trying to meditate around 2:00 A.M. A group of friends and I had agreed to wake up at that time each night for one month, and meditate for one hour. I had done this once before, and the sense of well-being that prevailed was profound. I was eager to do it again, However, the spirit was willing but the flesh was weak. I was only a few days into the monthlong process when I began to find it hard to stay awake for the whole hour.

I was meditating on the sofa beside the bed. I thought that perhaps I could slide down into the sofa just a little bit more, and still remain awake enough to continue praying and meditating. As I started to fall asleep, I suddenly heard a sound I'd heard many times before, a sound like a rushing wind. Then I felt Jesus' presence, even though, with my eyes remaining closed, I saw nothing but darkness. I experienced the intense energy of his breath upon my face. I felt deeply comforted and loved. Then I heard him ask, "What were you in Rome?" I was puzzled at first, having never been to Rome, but then a realization came from somewhere within me. I said, "I was two things!" I felt this was a confession of some kind of hypocrisy or deceit. (I had no idea then, or later, what it referred to.) But as soon as I mentally answered him, the energy and sound raised to a new level of intensity. It was hard to bear the intensity of the love emanating from him and coursing through me. I felt the intensification was his way of lovingly confirming the rightness of my response. I then lost consciousness and entered a dream that I've since forgotten. (G.S.S.)

I have puzzled over the content of these initiation experiences from a variety of angles, a task that I feel compelled to do whenever I have such momentous experiences. Content aside, however, we can see just how catalytic "mere" questions can be in the initiation process. By questioning us, Christ avoids a merely parental or teaching role in favor of eliciting responses from us that may be crucial to our spiritual maturation. Thomas Moore, author of *Care of the Soul* (Intervarsity Press, 2001), refers to this kind of relationship as a true *mentoring* relationship in which the mentor is committed to fostering the development of an inner authority rather than serving as a mere substitute for a person's own development:

. . . a deep father figure . . . settles into the soul to provide a sense of authority, the feeling that you are the author of your own life, that you are head of the household in your affairs.[23]

The next, richly detailed account reveals how Christ apparently works with individuals over a period of time to bring them eventually to a level of commitment and effectiveness far beyond their previous experience. The recipient, a Jewish psychotherapist, first experiences a series of awakening Christ encounters in which Jesus introduces himself to her in a comforting and loving manner. Then, once the relationship is established, she undergoes an initiation test: Essentially, Christ calls on her to go deeper into her spiritual practices, and she resists. Things get worse as she continues to resist the pressure to surrender to the process, until she eventually accepts and undertakes the work she is called to do. The relationship with Jesus is consolidated through her cooperative response to him, and she goes on to receive direct guidance from him on a later occasion.

In the interest of preserving the integrity of the account, S.K.'s multiple encounters are presented together in this chapter rather than including portions of the account in the chapters on awakening and instruction.

I am forty-nine and work as a psychotherapist. I also do some writing and have the apparent ability to do healing through laying on of hands.

I am Jewish, yet am strongly drawn toward the mystical and metaphysical. It took me about twenty-five years of seeking before I found a way to integrate Judaism with my other beliefs. Now, after the experiences I will describe to you, I find myself once more struggling to integrate something new.

Several years ago, I had an experience in which Jesus appeared to me several times during the course of a week. I would be doing something, such as going for a walk, and there he would be, looking at me in a loving way. There was an attitude, more than verbal communication between us. He seemed to be expressing in a kind, loving, gentle way, "What took you so long?" On a conscious level I wondered what that meant, yet at some deeper level I seemed to understand.

The experience left me feeling protected and safe along with an interest in Jesus. Being Jewish, I really hadn't learned very much about him.

In looking back at the experience, I am surprised at how casual I was about it. It seemed rather odd, but somehow natural. I didn't tell anyone about it at the time.

Three years later, my experience with him was markedly different. I had been going through a very busy, pressured week. At night I would get into bed quite exhausted. One morning during this time I was awakened by something or someone. It felt as if I had been shaken awake, but not in a very gentle way. It was 4:00 A.M.

I felt compelled to get up and meditate, but I didn't want to. I was too tired, but something wouldn't leave me alone. Almost against my will I got out of bed and went into the other room where I meditate. I really couldn't figure out why in the world I was doing this.

Soon after I entered a meditative state I was aware that to my right side was the presence of Jesus. This time his attitude was much more serious and I started receiving messages about ways I was needing to change. I was to meditate regularly (I'm rather lazy about meditating), do certain exercises first, and make some dietary changes.

The 4:00 A.M. awakenings continued for about a week or two. I was in a very uncomfortable state of mind and body. I was quite frightened. This was not the gentle, benign type of experience I had had with him previously. This was very serious. I felt out of control, as if I didn't have a choice.

My sense of reality was being threatened. How could Jesus appear to me? Why me of all people? Being Jewish made the whole experience even more disturbing. Where was this leading? I wondered if I was going crazy.

The lack of sleep coupled with the emotional stress took its toll. I started having problems with my body: swollen glands, sore throat, a lump under my arm, along with various aches and pains. I was one confused, frightened, unhappy woman.

Finally, I "made a deal" with Jesus that if he would stop awakening me at 4:00 A.M., I would make a commitment to meditate daily. With that, the awakenings stopped, but it took me approximately another month to regain my emotional and physical equilibrium, and I'm still processing the experience.

About two weeks into the experience, I suddenly started to feel sad for no reason that I could consciously identify. The sadness welled up in me and I often sobbed uncontrollably. These sobs were so intense that they wracked my whole body. The feeling that accompanied the tears was one of severe grief to have been separated from him for all of this time. The crying continued for a long time. Although the feeling of grief was clear, I couldn't understand what was happening. It was as if a different "me" or part of me was having these experiences and I was somehow not able to fully connect with that part.

The feeling I was left with was that in some way I knew Jesus or was close to him or believed in him at some distant time, and for some reason I was separated from him or perhaps turned away from him.

All of this has led to my working on myself psychologically and spiritually. I have been meditating much more regularly. I'm working at making the dietary changes, reading more spiritual material, and generally working harder at being more loving.

During the time of the "contact," I found myself becoming quite intuitive, and a number of my clients commented on how well the sessions were going. It was surprising to me since I was in such a state of exhaustion. I believe, at that time, I was infused with what I'll call the "Jesus energy." (S.K.)

This account has some possibly unsettling implications. For one, it suggests that Christ—at least in some cases—does not wait to be invited into our lives, but can enter unbidden to impose a relationship and an agenda upon the recipient. The transformative experience of Saul of Tarsus on the road to Damascus best exemplifies this type of unbidden encounter. While some of us might gladly submit to his will and envy those who have felt his tangible presence, others might feel violated by such an intrusion into their lives.

Jesus never inflicts pain on S.K. She begins to experience discomfort only as she "kicks against the pricks"—that is, as she resists a process of unfoldment that has been activated by her relationship with him. Then she feels relieved and empowered when she finally undertakes the prescribed course of action.

People who believe in a second coming of Christ are sometimes divided over how this event will take place. Some believe that Christ will manifest physically, leaving no doubt whatsoever that Christ has returned. Others believe that the second coming will be an internal experience, available only to those who have opened their hearts and minds to him. Even if this question could be answered, there is another, perhaps more difficult question: Will he manifest as the Jesus who walked the earth two thousand years ago or assume a more contemporary form that may go unnoticed by those looking for the biblical figure? The ability to recognize Christ in whatever form he appears is a crucial test of our understanding of his essential teachings. Having to look beyond the outward appearances of his coming may constitute one of the most fundamental initiation tests for those who profess to serve him. Essentially, it is a test that determines if Christ's conformance to our expectations is more important than Christ himself.

In the following account, the recipient, a forty-four-year-old speech pathologist who had the experience when he was twenty-six, encounters a Christ whose unconventional appearance is presented as a test in itself.

I had a dream in 1972 in which Christ appeared to me. Before the dream began there was a thought-transference experience. It wasn't an actual speaking voice, but it "spoke" and said, "This dream is a symbolic message not to be taken literally." The dream then began.

I received the message that Jesus was on a speaking tour of the United States and that he invited me to accompany him for two weeks. I accepted by returning a letter to him. I was subsequently sent to where he would be.

I felt like I was in the wrong place, but something reassured me I was in the right place. I knew that I just needed to look for him. I started wandering around this circus—that's why I didn't think I was in the right place; it was a circus. I soon found a sideshow tent with a sign proclaiming "Speaking Hourly! Jesus of Galilee! Come. See the Savior in Person! Admission Free." Again this voice came in the dream and reminded me this was all symbolic and not to be taken literally. I went inside the tent. The tent was empty but there was a stage up front and there was a stagehand there. I explained to him I was supposed to meet with Jesus and that he had invited me. As soon as I said that the stage hand's face brightened up and he said, "Oh yes! he's expecting you. But the show is about to start so you'll have to wait until afterward."

People were coming in and just then Jesus came around a curtain and saw me just as I saw him. Although I knew it was him, I was surprised at his appearance. Instead of the traditional Christ figure, he was wearing a gray pinstriped suit. He was bald—his face didn't look like the traditional Jesus face. Actually, he resembled my uncle Ed. I knew unquestioningly, however, that it was him. He greeted me and apologized for having to rush right into the perform-ance, I guess you'd call it. He gave me a glass of something to drink—lemonade or something.

After a few moments an announcer walked out on stage and said, "The show is about to begin. And now here he is— the one and only—Jesus, the Christ." It kind of reminded me of Johnny Carson's introduction. He began to speak. His words to me were like gold, but I don't remember the specifics of what he said. I just remember I was hanging on every word. After a few moments one fellow in the back of the tent said, "Oh, what is this?! I came to see a show, not to hear a lot of talk." And Jesus very tactfully replied that he was free to leave at any time. Jesus continued. Several others got up and left, grumbling and muttering. There was obvious skepticism, but some were really impressed. Others showed no doubt. One large fat lady was just beaming as he spoke. Over half had left since he started. Then there was a question and answer session, and other people left. Details are vague, but I know that I accompanied him for what seemed like two weeks.

He didn't always say the same thing. He seemed to tailor what he was saying to the needs of the particular people. Over the course of the two-week period, I noticed that the fat lady was frequently there in the front row. I also began to notice another man—it was hard not to notice him—who had bright red hair and wore a loud plaid jacket and orange pants. He seemed to appear quite frequently. I was concerned that he might be some evil or satanic influence. I said to Jesus, "Master, who is that man?" He replied, "You know, but not at this time," and just smiled. Finally, I asked him why he looked so different. He said, "Of course everyone would come to see me if I descended from the clouds in a white robe with angels attending, but that is not my purpose. I'm here to separate the wheat from the chaff. Those who truly know me will recognize me in Spirit—the rest will not know me. In this way I am gathering my true followers." Again I was told by the voice in the dream that the setting of the dream was symbolic—not to be taken literally. (S.P.)

It is interesting to note that the two figures other than the dreamer who remain committed to Christ have physically undesirable qualities—obesity and tasteless dress—upon which a more shallow individual might have rejected them. They, too, contrast with the "ideal" follower even as the Christ in the dream contrasts with the "ideal" Jesus figure. The whole thrust of the experience seems designed to test the dreamer's ability to look beyond super-ficial appearances, and give him further reason to suspend judgment on the basis of appearances. Thus, we can see that initiation goes beyond the mere assessment of the recipient. It also facilitates a strengthening of the very capacity it is designed to measure.

S.P. had no trouble seeing Christ behind his ordinary appear-ance. But what happens when we are faced with an *extraordinary* image that holds a great deal of allure, but which may ultimately be "less than the best"? Years ago I had the occasion to tell my friend and mentor, Dr. Herbert Puryear, about a series of UFO dreams that I had been experiencing. They were full of light and promise, and I was rather pleased with them. However, he asked, "Why do you settle for that?" I became irritated, a sure sign he was on to something. I knew he thought that I was limiting the experience, and that I could elect to encounter Christ instead. Although the following Christ encounter dream happened years later, it still points out a problem I was having in allowing the light to become as personal as it might.

At my father's business, I was looking out the side door toward the business across the street. I saw a UFO hovering about fifteen feet above the ground—brilliant red, flashing on and off. A friend was on the ground to the left of it. She said to me, "When are you going to see this for what it really is? You see it in two dimensions. When will you see it in three?" I looked again at the UFO carefully, and then saw Jesus standing between the craft and my friend. He was dressed in a white robe and headband. He and I began walking toward each other. We held out our hands to each other and clasped them. I was nearly overwhelmed by his presence, his love.

I then began to realize that I was dreaming. I was careful as I looked into his eyes to maintain the highest thoughts, believing that my thoughts had a determining influence on sustaining the contact. He held my gaze with a strong, loving expression. I noticed a similarity between his face and a painting that I'd seen before. As we parted, I went back and found another friend, whom I told about the experience. I told her about how he looked, and she was able to recall the painting that I was thinking about. I wondered if I could take her back and see Jesus with her. (G.S.S.)

It is interesting that my friend refers to the UFO as less than the three-dimensional, personal manifestation of Jesus. It is common to think otherwise—that God's personhood is merely our human, if not infantile, projection onto an impersonal deity. But not everyone thinks that the abstract is preferable, or even more true than the personal expressions of the divine. C.S. Lewis, in particular, speaks eloquently about the value of both:

> *This talk of "meeting" is, no doubt, anthropomorphic; as if God and I could be face-to-face, like two fellow creatures, when in reality he is above me and within me and below me and all about me. This is why it must be balanced by all manner of metaphysical and theological abstractions. But never, here or anywhere else, let us think that while anthropomorphic images are a concession to our weakness, the abstractions are the literal truth. Both are equally concessions; each singly misleading, and the two together mutually corrective.... What soul ever perished for believing that God the Father really has a beard?* [24]

It is probably true that most of us are better at experiencing God in one way or the other—either abstractly or personally. If so, then an initiation that we may each face as we approach the experience of the divine is to see the *divine from the other perspective*—in order to humbly acknowledge the other half of a paradoxical truth.

A fifty-four-year-old university theology professor tells of a Christ encounter that took place during his college years. The Christ encounter actually occurred following a series of preliminary experiences, which seemed to test him and prepare him for the eventual encounter.

This is the account of a unique happening in my life, while at Howard University, during my college years (1954–58); it was 1957 when I had the following religious experience.

I had been secretly communing with God in the form of Christ; that is, using an abandoned "Bleeding Heart" portrait of him as a focus for my prayers. I lit a candle and knelt before the portrait in the basement of Cook dormitory. Eventually, the dormitory director discovered me in my secret place and, to my surprise, asked if he could join me in prayer. For a while we communed there together. In those days, I was deeply into a form of Christ-mysticism. Christ became my daily object of adoration, and the wind became the Spirit of God against my face.

One day it so happened that I came to commune with God seven times. Although I do not recall the context of every event of communion, it all began at the suggestion of a rather verbose but brilliant young idealist that several of us gather at 6:00 A.M. in front of the library to pray for the state of the world. It was barely light when I got there. No one else came.

I was sad, but I prayed anyway; and just when I was about to leave, a strange wind came upon the leaves on the ground and gathered them around my feet. Perhaps this is not an unusual thing, but at the time it seemed that God was saying "Hello!" I returned to the dorm.

Later that day my girlfriend and I went to the chapel to pray together. We had resolved to have no sexual relations before marriage; and we shared the challenge of resisting the urge together through prayer and mutual confession.

Far into the evening, I was alone in my room when three students, all drinkers, dropped by and asked to come in. I obliged them, but soon they were making fun of what they perceived to be my consistent religiosity. They took my Bible and began tossing it around among themselves. I instinctively reached for it but to no avail, as they taunted me about my religious faith and my overheard verbal witness to the wonder of Christ.

Finally, when left alone, I prayed before I went to sleep.

Sometime between 3:00 and 4:00 A.M., I was lying on my right side, and opened my eyes. Before me was standing a barefooted person in a long garment, the upper part of whom I could not really see. I intuitively sensed that this was neither an ordinary figure nor an ordinary occurrence. For the figure—who I sensed was male—took his hand, which seemed unusually larger than any normal adult hand, and placed it on my shoulder. Then he gently squeezed my shoulder with his hand three times. I had the distinct feeling that the strength in those hands was so great that even a careless squeeze would have crushed my shoulder completely. I clearly knew I was being told not to despair or discontinue searching for truth. It was a deeply comforting spiritual experience that I knew was somehow related to the seven encounters with God during the previous day, although I did not think of this until later reflection upon the event.

I have meditated on why I was not able to see the face of the figure, and my thoughts have usually settled upon the idea that I was not spiritually ready to do so.

The next day when I met my special friend, I discovered what proved to be an amazing follow-up to the previous night's experience. I could greet her and talk of anything except the experience with Christ. When the moment came for me to share the experience with her, I could not speak a word of it, even though I tried. I reached the point of crying and facially giving the impression that I was choking on a bone in my throat. Every attempt to tell her of the experience ended in vain as we sat upon the steps of an out-of-the-way stairway of the library.

She reached out to help me as if I were being strangled at my every renewed effort to testify. And yet there was an almost immediate release from that constriction once I relented from making such an effort.

Eventually, I was able to testify of the event. I later realized that it was not merely a gesture of comfort but a form of anointing of my soul for a special work on behalf of the advancement of his kingdom on earth. I eventually entered the pastoral ministry and departed the little church I served in Arlington, Virginia, only after a memorably successful ministry. I had been called, ultimately, to enter academia (what I tend to call the "Teaching Ministry"). To this day, that experience stands uniquely among all my expe-

riences with God as the most significant, long-lasting, and confirming one that I have come to treasure. (W.B.)

It is significant that in each of the events that he could recall, W.B. faced a challenge and then responded to it with prayer and apparent acceptance. We get the sense that he could have stopped the initiation process at any point by simply succumbing to ordinary, understandable reactions to the disappointments or trials he faced. Did W.B. earn the visitation from Christ, or did he simply remove the barriers which normally prevent a person from experiencing an ever-present greater reality? The question goes to the heart of how one understands the role of Christ in the initiation process. Is he *active* as a judge and initiator? Or is he simply standing at the door beckoning—waiting for us to remove what stands in the way?

Given the culmination of W.B.'s initiation process, we can look back on the earlier stages of his struggles and appreciate the meaningfulness of the tests that arose. Indeed, when an encounter with Christ follows a series of unpleasant, testing situations, we can retrospectively see the design operating in what was previously unpleasant and unwanted challenges. The encounter with Christ at the end of a testing process serves to remind us to look upon the difficult tests in our lives as avenues to deeper communion with God rather than "punishments" that befall us for no apparent reason.

Listen! I am standing at the door, knocking;
if you hear my voice and open the door,
I will come in to you and eat with you,
and you with me.
Revelation 3:20

7

Instruction

"Giveth to me all your pain and sorrow.
You will be persecuted no more."
K.S.

THE POSSIBILITY THAT CHRIST HIMSELF PROVIDES instruction to individuals is an awesome prospect. Undoubtedly, few of us consider this likely to happen to us. We remain convinced that we will have to "go it alone," deriving instruction and piecemeal guidance from less lofty sources. In the accounts we examine in this chapter, however, we will see experiential evidence that Christ may, indeed, provide spiritual instruction to ordinary individuals.

In the following accounts, Christ teaches the recipient an important truth that needs to be acknowledged and applied in his or her life. In most cases, Christ does not address the practical issues that the recipient faces in his everyday life. Instead, he tends to convey instruction of a global nature that the recipient can subsequently apply in a variety of related areas.

In this first account, a woman receives a revelation about the purposefulness of her suffering. At the time, she was twenty-seven and had just come through a series of very difficult situations with her health, career, and relationships. The experience provided instruction to her that wasn't related just to one specific problem, but instead was more universal in meaning. Christ taught her about the crucifixion and how it relates to her life. By referring to his own tragic death as "positive," he helped her appreciate the meaningfulness of some of her own struggles. Significantly, Christ does not specifically cite the aspects of her life which correspond to her own "cross," but gives her the opportunity to conduct her own life review and arrive at her own conclusions.

I had a visitation from Jesus on March 6, 1987. It was not a dream. I actually saw him standing alongside the bed. He was wearing a white robe and a red sheath draped over his shoulder. He had a beard, mustache, and long, light brown hair. His physical appearance was what we imagine it to be.

Anyway, while Jesus was by my left side, I was lying on my back with my head propped up and my eyes wide open. We looked at each other, and as I gazed into his clear blue eyes, he said: "L., everything that happened to you, yes, was negative. But look at it this way."

Jesus extended his left arm out as an indication for me to look in that direction. I turned my head, looked toward his hand, and saw a movie in the air. As I was viewing the movie, I noticed that there were crowds of people along both sides of the road. The crowd from the movie and I (in bed) observed a gentleman who was dressed in shabby red and white garments. He looked physically weak and exhausted as he walked down a road, because he was carrying a wooden cross upon his shoulder and back. Then it dawned on me that I was watching Jesus' own personal story of that very day he changed the world for all mankind.

Right at that moment of understanding, the Jesus alongside my bed asked, "You see what happened to me?" as his hand extended toward the movie. "Yes," he continued, "it was negative," and his hand reached into the movie. Then, at the very moment he took the cross off his own back from the movie, he said, "But actually it was positive."

Jesus removed the tiny cross from the movie, turned around, and faced me. However, the cross in Jesus' hand had transformed into a black addition sign, the size of a baseball.

For a few moments, Jesus held the black cross in front of me; then he said, "This cross is positive."

I looked intently at the black plus sign as he continued.

"L., what happened to you was actually positive."

While I looked at Jesus beside me, I thought about the meaning behind both Jesus' story in the movie and the black cross he held in his hand. My thoughts quickly reviewed all that I had gone through; I had received a complete under-standing as to why the adverse events happened to me. Even though I had physically and emotionally suffered, these hardships were actually a spiritual gain. These losses were for my soul's growth here on earth. I thought how fortunate I was to experience these negative situations in this lifetime. I was so thankful that Jesus came to me and grateful for his healing, by answering my questions.

When Jesus knew that I was finished with my interpretation of the "big picture," he took my left hand and held it in his, saying, "Here, I want you to wear this cross." Jesus placed the black cross in my hand.

I definitely knew that Jesus placed the cross in my hand for I felt two sensations. One, I could feel the weight of the cross (his cross), which was unbearably heavy to hold; and second, the cross was like a hot iron on my palm. My hand was scorched. I had to fan myself from the burning heat. Jesus vanished.

Exactly one year later to the date, I was instructed through a dream to look at my left hand. I did so. There in the palm of my hand I saw a red raised scar of the sign of the cross. The same cross that Jesus placed in my hand upon his visitation. When I awoke from my dream that morning, I looked at my hand but there was no scar. However, I did trace the lines from my palm and sure enough, there were two: one horizontal, the other vertical. Today, my palm lines show that there is a cross.

I am greatly honored that Jesus himself came to me. Sometimes I just wonder. There is not a day that goes by that I don't think of his visitation and what it represents in my life. When I look at my hand it reminds me of Jesus walking to Calvary, and what he said to me that very night: "You see what happened to me! Yes, it was negative. But actually it was positive. This cross is positive." (L.B.)

In this moving account, Jesus takes L.B. beyond a superficial assessment of her suffering into a profound new understanding of her life based on its parallels with his own suffering and death. He does not offer specific guidance concerning the directions she should take on the basis of the deeper understanding. It is as though the experience is sufficient to awaken in her a response to life that will affect numerous situations.

Similarly, I experienced this type of indirect instruction in two Christ encounter dreams which were separated by several years. In both, Jesus spoke to me in symbolic or metaphorical imagery about my life, much as he did in his enigmatic parables. These experiences still serve usefully as somewhat mysterious and indirect statements against which I compare my current choices and attitudes.

In a dream that I had twenty-five years ago, Christ spoke to me about the Pearl of Great Price:

> *I am in a dark room. The only thing I can see at first is Jesus standing in front of me. He is discussing the Pearl of Great Price, as though it is something I should seek. He is also saying that I must take care not to collect more than one pearl, for then I would be unable to close the lid of the treasure chest that contains it. I see a treasure chest in my mind's eye which is stuffed with pearls and cannot be closed.*
>
> *I then see C., my fiancée at the time. I conclude that Jesus is talking about life partners, and that I should settle on one rather than keep my options open. I say to her, "I guess this means we should be married." I take a sip from a wine glass, then give it to her. It is as though we are consecrating our decision. (G.S.S.)*

In the parable of the Pearl of Great Price, Jesus compares the pearl to the kingdom of heaven. He tells of a merchant who, upon finding the pearl, is willing to sell everything to have it.

Again, the kingdom of heaven is like a merchant in search of fine pearls; on finding one pearl of great value, he went and sold all that he had and bought it. (Matthew 13:45–46)

It was understandable that I interpreted Jesus' instruction to me in a very specific way during the course of the dream. While he was probably referring to my need to commit myself *in general*, I interpreted his words specifically in terms of human relationships.

This experience demonstrates how easily we can look for specific guidance from a spiritual experience that is intended to address a general theme. After all, Jesus did not say, "Marry this person." That would have made the decision for me. No, he was saying, "*You* need to decide what is most important, and then *you* need to stick with it." I came to see the experience as a reminder of a strong tendency of mine as a young man: to preserve too many options without becoming singularly committed to anything.

In a second dream, Jesus spoke to me concerning the same general problem, again offering spiritual instruction steeped in metaphor.

I am with Jesus and his disciples on top of a high hill. He is washing our feet. I am deeply moved and honored by his gesture. When he comes to me, he speaks to me while he is washing my feet. He says that I have a problem with my breathing. He says that I need to learn to breathe in a deeper, different way. Once I learn this, he says, I will not have to breathe as often. (G.S.S.)

Immediately following this dream, I thought Jesus had been referring literally to my physical breathing. But when I had trouble seeing the validity of this advice, I realized that Jesus was probably addressing my need for spiritual "breathing," or deep devotional practice, since I had fallen down in my regular prayer and meditation practice at the time.

As time went on, the spiritual instruction of this experience seemed even more global, and I began to see a link between the themes of the first and second dreams. Eventually, I realized that Jesus had again referred to the same problem: a scattered, uncommitted outlook. In the previous dream about the Pearl of Great Price, the lesson was to focus and to make a singular commitment. In the second experience, it was to slow down, to savor my experience with greater depth and quality, and to place less emphasis on quantity. And this, I realized, could be applied to breathing, to meditation, to relationships, and to any number of other issues in my life.

Why does Jesus speak so indirectly in these accounts? Why doesn't he just tell us what we need to know? Actually, we should not be surprised, because this is exactly the way Jesus spoke when he walked the earth two thousand years ago. His followers and critics alike were always looking for simple answers to complex questions, but Jesus frustrated them by using metaphors and imagery to convey a much deeper answer than they could grasp at the moment.

With this in mind, the following account makes perfect sense. A six-year-old girl had a dream the day before Easter, in which Christ spoke to her in symbolic terms. One can see how his use of imagery conveyed information about her parents that may have been impossible to communicate through language alone.

I had my own personal encounter with Christ in a dream at the age of six, the night before Easter. The dream has stayed with me my whole life, and is as real now as it was then.

I dreamed that I was in the living room of the house my family lived in then when Jesus appeared to me. I was so awestruck, and my heart was touched because he had shown up for me. I immediately ran into the kitchen where my father, brother, and my new stepmother were. I told them that Jesus was in the living room, so they followed me back there, but he wasn't there, so they returned to the kitchen. When I turned around, there he was again. I ran back into the kitchen screaming to my family once again, "Jesus is in the living room." They were reluctant to leave the kitchen this time but did so at my insistence. Jesus was nowhere in sight. Again my family made fun of me, and this time they seemed really angry with me; they returned to the kitchen again.

When I turned around, there he was again. He lovingly told me that only I could see him, not my family. Then Jesus took me by the hand to the kitchen to show me something. He pointed to the Easter eggs that my parents were decorating for Easter. My parents were carefully putting poison in the eggs that were to be put in my Easter basket for Sunday. I was stunned with what I saw; my sadness was so great that I could hardly breathe. Jesus then told me lovingly that I would be all right, and he instructed me just not to eat the eggs.

The next day was Easter, and my parents did not understand why their little girl would not touch the truly beautiful Easter eggs my mother had made during the night.

This dream helped me so much as I was growing up. My father was very violent and both physically and verbally abusive to the extreme. This dream made me see my parents as the disturbed persons they were, and I did not take the harmful things they said about me as truth. So I grew up feeling that there was something inherently wrong with my parents—unlike most abused children, who end up feeling, as the result of habitual abuse, that there is something wrong with them. Though I have needed therapy because of this tormented past, I was able to develop healthier psychologically as a result of my encounter with Jesus.

I feel I was spared years of therapy that would have been otherwise necessary to put back together a shattered personality, if indeed this could have been done at all. The presence of Christ has been with me my whole life. I'm now forty-five. I feel so grateful. (P.L.)

It is remarkable that P.L. was able to translate the concreteness of the Easter egg imagery into an overall cautious attitude toward whatever her parents subsequently tried to impose upon her. And yet she was obviously able to remain flexible enough in her interpretation not to reject *everything* that they would give her from that day onward. Even children who receive such instruction seem to know how to interpret and apply Christ's symbolic communications. It may be that this knowledge is subtly imparted to the recipient during the experience itself.

P.L.'s experience served to prevent her from being hurt as much as she could have been by parents who were incapable of nurturing her. Christ essentially told her not to rely on them as much as a child would normally do. In contrast, Christ tells another little girl to reach out to assailants who have nearly beaten her to death. With advice that goes against everything that one might expect, Christ urges her to appeal to a compassion that has been totally absent in their vicious treatment of her.

When I was nine years old, I was taken and brutally attacked by three men for several hours. My whole inner being was begging to die in order to escape the physical pain I was experiencing. At one point I was in a semiconscious state and I could hear the men talking about how to dispose of my "dead" body. I could not speak or move to tell them I wasn't dead yet. I felt my body in the process of dying and was glad that I could finally escape the pain.

Then I became aware that I could choose whether I lived or died. When I realized that I had a choice, I couldn't make up my mind. I had strong feelings for both life and death. A voice was telling me that time was running out and I had to make a decision soon, or it would be too late—I would be irreversibly dead.

As I considered never seeing my mommy and daddy again—and felt their grief and sadness over not having me with them—I chose to live.

After I made my choice I heard a voice telling me to move my body so the men would know that I was still alive. I could not move even a muscle on my own and then Jesus appeared to me, standing by my right foot (I was on the ground). He reached down and moved my legs and one of the men saw me move and took compassion on me. The man wrapped me in a blanket, took me to his dwelling, cleaned me up and took me home.

I did not see Jesus' face. I just knew who he was. I say "he," but what I saw was a large, gentle white figure. There were no words—just an atmosphere of deep, deep caring and a wave of peace filled my body. All my pain and bruises and cuts felt healed.[27]

Christ knew something about this brutal situation that few people would have considered: that compassion could be aroused in one of the men, no matter how evil he had acted toward the little girl. For most of us, the most difficult aspect of Jesus' example was his acceptance of his enemies and his understanding of their essential goodness in spite of their harsh treatment of him. His words, "Father, forgive them; for they do not know what they are doing" (Luke 23:34), were uttered while he was on the cross and the soldiers were casting lots for his garment. This depth of love is so inconceivable that most of us tend to exempt ourselves from emulating his example. But this incredible love was not a small part of his life, it was in everything he did. In the above account, taken from Morton Kelsey's *Resurrection*, we find this love manifested again, this time saving the life of a little girl who was encouraged to reach out for love in the most unexpected place.

The next two accounts suggest that some instruction may be so subtle, so incomprehensible or inconceivable, that it simply cannot be recalled. The recipient, a sixty-five-year-old woman who had the experience when she was fifty-six years old, was undergoing surgery at the time of the first experience.

Sometime during surgery, I was floating very high in dark blue space. I did not have the physical body I have on earth. I chuckled at how small I was. I was all lit up like a tiny light. I had little arms and hands and could see behind me without turning or looking behind. I was delightfully happy. I then floated over the hospital. The surgery is on the second floor and my room was on the sixth floor, the top floor. I looked down into the surgery room just as though the upper floors were not there. I chuckled again at how small everyone was from my vantage point. I knew that it was me on the operating table.

Then I thought, Are you sure? Just by thinking this, I backed up and went sideways where I could see at a better angle. That was me all right. I then went at a rapid rate of speed back to the operating table. I was not concerned with anyone or anything except a glowing golden light in the shape of an arc over my head. . . .

I saw the surgeon and can tell you exactly what he was wearing and what he looked like. However, I had no interest again in what was going on as the upper right portion of the room was replaced with the same dark blue space I had been floating in. In the upper center of the blue space was a tiny white spot, or little white light. This light was getting larger and larger. Then I realized it was approaching at a rapid rate of speed, and it took on the shape of a human.

From approximately fifteen to eighteen feet away the figure stopped. It was Christ—when you look into those eyes you have no doubt. Without speaking, he communicated a message. I cried several times, "I don't know how, I don't know how." I tried to get up to go to him but found I was strapped to the table above the waistline by a white two-inch strap. I told him again, "I don't know how."

All of a sudden all my anguish and anxiety left and I was filled with peace—then off to the right appeared crystal-clear mountaintops which seemed to surround a valley that was glowing with light. From this valley came beautiful music like a whole choir of angels singing a capella. I continued to hear beautiful classical music right up to the time I woke up in my room the following morning.

I immediately told my husband, "I saw God." His remark was, "Well, if you say so."

Later, another encounter occurred in a dream. I woke up remembering that Christ spent the whole night talking to me, giving me important information about something I was supposed to do. But when I woke up, I forgot everything he said! I was so distraught that all day long I begged that I please dream of him once more and hear his instructions again so that I could remember them.

Well, I awoke the next day with the same exact feeling, and again I had forgotten everything he said. I decided that whatever he said went into my subconscious and perhaps I wasn't ready to hear it yet. I can only add that each time I feel his presence, an indescribable feeling comes over me and it is always a warm and loving one. (A. R.)

Does the instruction we receive in the Christ encounter need to become a fully conscious realization? Or can this guidance operate just as effectively on an unconscious level, motivating us without our full knowledge of it doing so? In other words, if we forget what he tells us, do we lose the benefit of his guidance?

From the evidence of the following Christ encounter, it may be that knowing too much about our future can actually short-circuit the process of our unfoldment. In this dramatic encounter, a young girl meets Jesus in what is apparently the afterlife and is granted a vision of her past and future, only to have the future blocked from her memory later on.

When I was ten years old, I had acute appendicitis and had to undergo surgery. As they administered the anesthesia, I started to feel like I was falling into a dark well. The nurses seemed to be getting farther away, and their voices became mere echoes.

Then I began observing myself from the ceiling, and heard a loud buzzing or whistling sound. Instantly, I was in some other place. I could hear a noise that sounded like iron or metal doors scraping together.

A man came up to me and said, "Come with me." He put his hand on my right arm and gently led me up what seemed to be a dark tunnel. My feet were not touching the ground, but I felt like I was walking nonetheless. I was very scared, and my senses were very vivid and sharp. I was aware that I had been in surgery, and that somehow I had arrived in a different place.

I didn't see any light, but about halfway up I heard children laughing and playing as if in a gigantic playground. That comforted me a lot.

Eventually, someone met us and stopped us. I heard a man ask my escort who I was, and then he said to wait there. One other person waited with me. The other man went away and came back and said, "You'll have to take her back. We're not ready for her yet." As I turned around, I blacked out.

The next thing I knew I was being taken through a gate and up a sidewalk. I had no control. I was being led in a firm but loving manner. I had no desire to go my own way. I was led to a room that was snow white. I was told to wait because someone wanted to speak with me. The room was made of marble or glass, and it glowed. The light was soft on my eyes.

There was a throne or a chair with three or four steps all around it. It was made out of the same material as the rest of the room. I sat down on the bottom step and waited. Someone *came in from the right. He walked up and sat down on the chair. He was dressed in a long white robe. There was something so powerful about his presence that I knew he had to be Jesus.*

When he looked at me, his eyes said it all. The most powerful kind of love completely penetrated me. It was like liquid love being poured through my whole being. It was beautiful. (The feeling comes back when I talk about it, and I'm feeling it even now.)

He spoke to me without opening his mouth. I felt the love. His message was, in essence, "You are precious to me." I can't describe how I felt then. He said I wouldn't be allowed to stay there, but he told me in general terms about some of the things that I had to do, but he couldn't tell me exactly what. He said, "If I told you exactly what you needed to do, you would hurry and get it done, and it wouldn't turn out the same. Things have to go in their own time." He also told me I would forget some of the things that I was being told.

Then he asked me to get up and walk across the room, where I looked into something like a sink or a box. It was like TV, only more vivid. He showed me things from the time I was a baby right on until the present. I had been adopted as a baby. I was unloved and unwanted. He showed me the past and the future. At one point after looking at the future, I felt an overwhelming sense of joy and happiness, but the future was entirely blocked from my memory once I came back.

I was afraid that I'd never be able to come back to him. He said if I wanted to come back I had to obey his commands and to love others.

Then after he showed me everything, another person led me back down the tunnel. When I started to head back, everything went blank. I knew nothing else until I awoke in the hospital. I was immediately aware of what had happened to me. It felt so good to be inside my body again.

"Thank God, she's awake!" the nurse said when I woke up. I was in the hospital for over a month after that. My appendix had burst.

I carried this story in private for years. I wasn't allowed to speak of it. Since that time, I have been more aware of people, and how vulnerable they are. I am more sensitive and in tune with how they feel. Everybody matters. Everyone is loved and precious to the Lord.

Often I hear my Lord saying, 'I'm here, child. I'll never leave you." (C.L.)

In our search for spiritual guidance, many of us focus on what the future holds for us. We would like to be saved from endless trial and error, so we consult various oracles—dreams, priests, or counselors—hoping to be told how to save ourselves time and trouble. But apparently, even the highest source of instruction—God himself—withholds from us what is in our best interest not to know. He wants us to undergo the journey, not to simply arrive at our final destination. In C.L.'s experience, she is assured of Jesus' love, and she knows what she must do to find her way back to him. Everything else, it seems, is up to her to find out.

Many of the previous accounts are characterized by instruction expressed indirectly through metaphors and symbols—or even information that is withheld from conscious awareness—but Christ can also deliver very direct, practical instructions. In this next

account, Christ manifests to C.M., ostensibly to urge her to offer
professional help to a minister she doesn't even know.

*I was twenty-one years old, and was living in a room by
myself in a private home. One night I woke up and saw a
dim light over in the corner of the room. The light grew
larger and brighter. A voice came from the light, calling my
name. I couldn't see any person. But I asked, "Who are you,
and what do you want?" I was afraid, and knew there was
nothing in that part of the room to account for the light.
Then in the light I saw the face and form of Jesus. He was
wearing a long white robe and his feet were bare, a few
inches off the floor.*

*He said, "I have work for you to do." He then asked me if
I would serve him, and I said, "Yes, Jesus. What do you want
me to do?" I felt very honored to be called to serve him. He
said for me to call a certain man, who was a minister, and
that he would tell me what to do.*

*I didn't know the man, but I called him the next day and
told him that Jesus had told me to call him. He wasn't
surprised. He asked me to come over to his church on
Saturday morning, which I did. As we talked, he said that
Jesus had promised to send the help he had been praying for.
When I told him where I worked—in the public relations
department of a large publishing company—he knew that I
was the one who was sent to do the work. So he instructed me
in what he wanted me to do, and I helped him for several
weekends. When the job was over, he thanked me and said it
had been helpful to many people.*

*Soon afterward, Jesus appeared to me again in my
room, and thanked me for my work. While I have heard his*

voice since then, I have never seen him again in that way.
(2nd C.M.)

It is surprising, perhaps, that Jesus manifests to C.M., not to commission her to start a new movement or to make pronouncements to the public, but to get her to help someone with a project that will benefit many others. The apostles were frequently guided by the risen Christ on very practical issues in the days immediately following Jesus' crucifixion. While it might be easy to believe that he would assist his closest friends on such day-to-day matters, it might be hard to believe that Christ would manifest himself today in small-scale situations to individuals who are in no position to effect widespread changes in today's complex world.

We see Christ again exhibiting an indirectness and subtlety in the following account, which goes to the heart of the dreamer's neglected sense of humor about the spiritual path. He had been active in the Methodist church during high school but had drifted away during his college years. In graduate school, his roommate was a philosophy major and the two of them had many long discussions concerning religion, God, and related issues. He began to meditate and take spiritual growth very seriously. By his own account, he became overly pious and much too serious. Being religious was important to him, but that seemed to mean giving up fun and frivolous activity. He had the following dream:

I was attending class in a large auditorium on campus. The room had a capacity for a hundred or more students and reminded me of the type of classroom where freshman history was taught. I was sitting in the middle of the room and there were only a few empty seats remaining in class. Class had just begun and the lecturer for the day was God. I was listening intently to everything God was saying (although I remembered nothing later) when I heard the rear door to the auditorium open.

I thought to myself, "Who could possibly be coming in late to God's class?" When I turned to look, it was Jesus coming down the aisle toward me with a smile on his face. He took a seat one row behind me and three seats to my left. I was totally amazed that Jesus would be late to class and still be smiling. As he sat down he looked over to me and winked. I turned around quickly and was astounded! I kept saying to myself, "Jesus winked at me! I can't believe it, Jesus actually winked at me!" Then I awoke with an incredible feeling of peace and joy.

As I pondered the meaning of the dream the next morning, I began to realize that being spiritual did not mean maintaining a serious and pious manner, but enjoying the life we are privileged to have while continuing to listen to God's will and practice the lessons he teaches us. The dream was telling me to "lighten up"—even Jesus winks and has a sense of humor. That dream has meant much to me during the past twenty years and whenever I begin to take my role too seriously, invariably my mind recalls that dream and gently reminds me to "lighten up." (H.C.)

Some readers might find Jesus' humor out of line with the seriousness he exhibits in the New Testament accounts. Since we know so little about how Jesus lived and interacted with his friends, there is no way to know if he joked and laughed a great deal or maintained a serious attitude throughout his life. My friend and mentor, Hugh Lynn Cayce, had several Christ encounters during his lifetime. When he told of them in his many lectures on Christ, he often said that Jesus always exhibited a sense of humor.

Similarly, in Betty Eadie's now-famous near-death experience, she, too, experienced Christ as a humorous, lighthearted being.

I'll never forget the Lord's sense of humor, which was as delightful and quick as any here—far more so. Nobody could outdo his humor. He is filled with perfect happiness, perfect goodwill.[28]

In support of this view of Christ, T.W. experiences Christ appearing to her and playfully mimicking her solitary dance. But after joining with her in play, he silently instructs her on a neglected dimension of her life—spiritual practice.

I was in a wide-open playground with a merry-go-round. It was a sunny day and I was blissfully dancing around, feeling immense love toward everyone and imagining world peace. I sang out "I love God" at the top of my lungs. It was out of tune, because I couldn't sing, but I didn't care. In my peripheral vision, there was a figure of a man also happily dancing, trying to mimic my movements. This was very amusing to me, but I just kept flailing around doing my own thing. I kicked up my leg, and saw his leg and sandal go up from under the edge of a white robe.

I felt a great sense of friendship and love toward this person, but turned to continue dancing by myself and focusing on world peace. Before I could turn, however, he gently grabbed me by my forearms. I found myself looking straight into the glorious, sparkling eyes of Jesus. He was radiant, joyous, and laughing, and I felt complete love, acceptance, and fun.

Then it slowly dawned on me that this was actually Jesus Christ! I became slightly self-conscious and vaguely realized that I had been singing out of tune and dancing around like an idiot in front of him.

Still smiling and holding my arms, he led me closer to the ground, until we were almost in a meditative position. (T.W.)

T.W. had just fallen into a depression after enjoying a long period of relative bliss and joy. When she plummeted into the pit of despair, the dream came to let her know that she hadn't done anything wrong, but that Jesus himself was leading her to go within, and to meditate. About this dream, she said, "He lovingly showed me how I had been out of attunement (singing out of tune) and could find greater attunement by going within (meditating). He was helping me to find peace within myself first, so that my ideal of world peace and love could be more fully realized."

The following moving account is an emotionally healing instructional encounter that gave the recipient, a twenty-seven-year-old woman at the time, the courage she needed to make changes in her life.

Around 1979, I was married and living in Austin, Texas. I had a B.F.A. in art, had worked as an assistant art director in advertising, and had opened a store in a hotel with imports I was bringing in from Hong Kong. I was successful in many ways, but my marriage of six years was failing. I was still spiritually oriented but not particularly "religious." I had been reared in the Catholic religion, but saw no particular importance in Christianity other than good ethical dogma on a par with Hinduism or Buddhism. I considered my "vow" of marriage very serious, but found my current condition intolerable. I felt unsure about leaving my husband at the time, but opted to try to "ride it out."

One morning I awoke and sat up in bed. My then-husband was still sleeping. The room took on an eerie grayish, misty glow. Before me, in full form, appeared the Lord, Jesus Christ. There was no question for me who this was. He spoke to me in words, but not words—more of a nonverbal, but somehow still verbal, communication. He told me to be at peace. He told me it was all right to divorce my then-husband. He bestowed tremendous peace on me. We just loved each other. He told me he would see me again before I died. And then he left. Needless to say, I was awed. I did not even consider myself a good or believing Christian at the time.

I remember laughing that no one would even believe this. I did proceed with my divorce about one year later. (S.L.K.)

It is probably true that when we feel loved, we are most likely to move off dead center and take some risks to grow beyond our stagnation. S.L.K. apparently needed to know that she had tried her best and could, with a clear conscience, move on. Today at forty-one, she is remarried and has two stepchildren.

Many scripturally committed individuals do not believe in divorce except in cases of adultery—the only exception cited by Jesus in Mark. They would find this account hard to accept, unless the husband's adultery could be established. Advocates of a scripturally consistent position would consider this experience obviously invalid and the Christ figure a clever embodiment of deceit. Exponents of a more liberal view could argue that Christ's teachings today would be somewhat different in order to adjust to the context of contemporary values.

Neither of these positions say anything about what the witness might contribute to the unfoldment of the experience. They are focused on the content of the experience, not the witness's own beliefs and biases, which might distort the content somewhat. From this position, one might say that S.L.K. ultimately inferred that Christ approved of her divorce, even though he may not have intended to take any stand on that matter. She wondered about this herself in her letter to me, asking, "Where does subjective and objective meet? All I can say is, 'I know what I know.'"

A woman who had recently left an abusive and unfaithful husband was grieving over her separation from her children. In her moving encounter with Jesus and Mary, she receives instruction that appears on the surface to offer her permanent relief.

In June of 1996, I left a long, painful marriage to an angry and hostile man. It was a difficult decision, because doing so meant I was also leaving behind my children; distance in miles was needed to protect not only my physical being, but my emotional and spiritual health as well. My daughter was off to college and my son, being a teenager, opted to stay with his father so he wouldn't have to leave his friends. I moved eight hundred miles away because I was offered a job in a publishing house connected to a spiritual organization. The support of my new friends and my daily spiritual practice were essential for me to have the strength to be separated from my children.

In September, I made a trip for the initial divorce proceedings. It was during this trip that my son adamantly stated that he wished to stay with his father, and he no longer wanted me to raise the question of his moving. It had been an ongoing discussion for several months. It was incredibly difficult for me to be at peace with this decision, but I knew I had no choice.

In the middle of the night the phone rang, and I reflexively jumped out of bed to answer it. Unfortunately, I had forgotten that I was on the top bunk in my daughter's dorm room, and I landed on my feet hard. A loud snap erupted from my knee, and for the remainder of the day, I suffered increasingly severe pain. Since it was clear that my son would not be joining me, I made arrangements to rent a truck and take the remainder of my belongings that had been in storage back with me.

After buying a knee brace at a sporting goods store, I spent the afternoon alone, loading the truck. Besides being physically difficult because of my injury, it was also emotionally painful. I felt as if with each box, with each piece of furniture that I lifted, I was reviewing my life. The baby clothes and my son's football helmet were the most difficult to handle. Somehow I drove the eight hundred miles the next day, with all of my belongings, to my new home.

Several weeks passed, and my knee was not healing. My doctor had recommended surgery to repair the torn ACL, but this was not an option. I lived alone, in a second-floor condo, with a dog, and I had to get to work each day. I relied on alternative methods of healing, including massage, laying on of hands, and castor oil packs.

In October, I participated in a conference featuring Matthew Fox, which was very spiritually uplifting and *allowed me to feel some hope for my life again. During a break, I took a walk along the beach and I came to realize that the pain in my knee was related to the "hole in my heart." Strangely, the pain was increasing again. I made arrangements to have a laying-on-of-hands by a healer I knew after the closing of the conference.*

I arrived at the woman's house and laid down on the table to settle in. I suddenly became aware of a presence in the room, but knew it was not my friend. She was in the next room.

I mentally asked who was there, and I knew it was Jesus. I was a bit disbelieving at first, but the peace and warmth I felt were undeniable. I settled in and trusted that anything that occurred had to be good.

My friend appeared and began praying with me before doing the healing. I said nothing about Jesus' presence. I closed my eyes and surrendered to the experience. Before long, I was aware of two sets of hands on me. My friend concentrated her touch on my knee, but Jesus' hands were on my heart. Then with my eyes still closed, I clearly saw him standing next to the table, looking down at me! Then I saw Mary, the Holy Mother, standing at my feet. She silently watched over me, holding my feet. By this time, I was crying. I felt as if Jesus was taking large chunks of pain from my chest. He leaned over and said to me, "Giveth to me all your pain and sorrow. You will be persecuted no more."

I was aware that I was not in my body, but with them in a different realm. I felt completely enveloped in their love, and I felt so completely "at home." I wanted to stay there with them, but I knew I had to go back to my body, which by this time was very cold. Slowly, I returned, sobbing so deeply—not from the pain of being apart from my children and at odds with my ex, but because I was separating from Jesus and Mary. My friend was a bit concerned since she felt the drop in my body temperature. After she wrapped me with a blanket, I told her briefly of my experience. It was difficult to tell. I just wanted to go home and be alone with it. I left there feeling very much "in love with God."

It's been four years since I had my first experience with Jesus (there have been several with both him and Mary since), and I've only now come to realize that his telling me to give him "all my pain and sorrow, and that I'd be persecuted no more," didn't mean I would no longer have to face life's difficulties. Instead, he was encouraging me to go to him during troubled times and to find peace within my relationship with him. I think I'm beginning to do that, and only wish I could have done it from the very moment he came to me. (K.S.)

Again we see that the instruction that Christ bestows reveals its deeper meaning as a person ponders it over time. Since we all yearn for relief from hardship, it would be tempting to interpret his words to K.S. as a guarantee against hostile and adverse conditions. And yet she eventually realizes that his guidance has less to do with ensuring her perpetual comfort than with securing a relationship with him that can sustain her through the hardships that she must inevitably face while living in this world.

The following dream of a twenty-seven-year-old man resembles the earlier dream of L.B. about the crucifixion. Again the recipient learns a profound truth about Jesus' death on the cross—that he lives. Interestingly, the man comes to this realization through the agency of a mediator, an angel who explains the significance of what he has witnessed.

I was lying in bed. It was morning so I got up and went to the kitchen and sat down at the table. As I looked out the window, I saw a cross in the garden with Jesus on it. I was really concerned about this and wanted to check to see if it was really him. I was able to look past the window and found myself outside (but not with a physical body). The air seemed to be in waves, as if the air was two thousand years old and liquid-like.

I was able to get very close to Jesus and wanted to know if the cross and Jesus were real. I was now right beside him. I could see him suffering terribly and I felt a lot of distress because he was hurting so much. He was dirty and bloody.

The problem was that the weight of his body caused his arms to be too stretched—because his hands were nailed to the cross. As he tried to lift his body up to relieve the pain a little, it caused even more pain. It was really difficult.

I then began to inspect him, as though through a microscope. As I went down over his body, I realized he was naked, and how awful that must be for him to be exposed like that— embarrassing. I felt so much shame that I withdrew and found myself back in the kitchen.

As I sat there wondering what I could do to help stop the suffering, an angel appeared from above. The angel had no form but was beautiful. The angel told me that he/she had been sent by God to tell me that I had been with Jesus before. . . .

I began to wonder at this and sat down. I heard a very loud, terrifying scream. I knew that it was over, Jesus had died, and I felt sorrow, guilt, and fear. As I thought about these things, the angel reappeared and told me that I shouldn't feel sad and guilty, but rather that I should be glad that Jesus died because by doing so he had gotten rid of sin— sorrow, guilt, fear, and doubt. The angel said that I should be happy. The angel left and I got up to go to the kitchen door that leads out to the backyard and garden. As I approached the door I looked out the window.

There I saw Jesus, and he was alive! And he was really very healthy looking. He said my name, but it wasn't my current name. It was another name, but I knew it was mine. He was smiling. I was so joyful to see him! It was sunny and I heard music. I felt full of joy.

Then I woke up. After this experience, my whole life changed for the better. (P. H.)

In this profound experience, P.H. is blessed with a direct experience of Jesus' death and resurrection. Not only does he witness the horror and humiliation of Jesus' final hours, but he enjoys the glory of his life resurrected.

As we have observed in other accounts, the appearance of an angel or spokesman alongside the Christ figure is by no means uncommon. This presence typically serves as an interpreter, or as a "bridge" between the recipient's human frame of reference and the deeper meaning of what is happening.

A friend of mine, who is an architect by training, has been involved for many years in giving lectures and teaching courses on meditation, prayer, and other aspects of the spiritual life. He had been invited to speak to a large conference for three consecutive mornings. Like speakers do from time to time, he failed to pace the presentation of his material to fit the time allotted; by the third morning, he was out of things to say.

Things went well on the first morning. My presentation proceeded smoothly, and for the workshop portion, I elected to use a guided reverie in which the participants were "guided" up a mountain path where they would meet the spiritual teacher that each anticipated.

On the second of three mornings, my presentation again flowed smoothly. After it was completed, I opened the floor for discussion. During an animated session with lots of questions and dialogue, I found to my horror that I had inadvertently gotten into the material that I'd planned to present the next day. I had presented it all and now had nothing more to present during the third morning segment. Since I was away from my resource material, I was completely unequipped to come up with anything new.

On the third morning, immediately upon rising, I took my Bible in hand, praying that I would be offered guidance for the morning. After a period of intense prayer for guidance, and a deep gratitude for God's immanence, I opened the Bible for guidance.

That was not to be! I opened the book and stared at disbelief as I found not a single clue about how to organize the third session. I became angry, and I told God about my anger. In effect, I said that this was his show, that he had brought me all the way to California from Texas, and this was certainly not the time to leave me helpless.

With that, I took a shower, still fuming with the Almighty because I felt so stranded, as it were, in midstream. While standing there with water streaming over me, all of a sudden I found myself on the mountain path walking excitedly up the mountain to meet my teacher. As I came around a curve, there stood Jesus—close by and as real as any person would appear to me in an ordinary physical experience.

He was radiant. His arms were outstretched, such that his pearl-gray robe moved softly in the breeze. His eyes were brilliant as he impaled my gaze. He smiled ever so gently as he said in the most loving tone, "Bring them to me." And then he was gone, and I was abruptly back in the shower.

Overwhelmed by the experience, I shook and I cried and I laughed. Later I thought, "Sure, that's easy for you to say. But how am I to do that?" Then slowly an idea came to me: I could use the same mountain walk reverie again, but give the participants a longer time to experience their own relationship to their teacher.

When I went to the session that morning, I decided to tell them what had happened, and how the solution for the morning had come to me. They were delighted to enter into the process again. The morning went swiftly, and the reverie was very intense. Afterward, there was no question in my mind that virtually every person there experienced "contact" with Christ in whatever form they allowed him to assume. (2nd J.D.)

J.D. receives a brief, intimidating set of instructions. But he not only hears the words, he *tastes firsthand the very thing that he must invite others to experience.* In other words, J.D. knows that Jesus' instructions are realistic, because his own experience is proof of it. Thus, he must have communicated a profound conviction as he led the audience through the reverie for the second time—a conviction that evidently created a context in which new, amazing things were suddenly possible for the participants.

In conclusion, we have seen that some individuals receive spiritual instruction in their Christ encounters—teaching that goes far beyond mere problem-solving for day-to-day decisions. In these accounts, we can see how Christ expresses the import of his teaching through metaphor, imagery, and powerful emotional experiences which convey the essence of the teaching. On one hand, one can breathe a sigh of relief that these teachings generally restate the enduring truths already familiar to Christianity. But they are embedded in a context of imagery and feeling that alludes to subtleties beyond the recipient's conscious understanding. Thus, these Christ encounters offer a meaningful, somewhat mysterious springboard for future choices and actions—a life-reorganizing focus which never loses its relevance nor becomes fully understood.

As the reader has seen, these accounts do not say much about prophecy; nor do they reveal previously hidden spiritual truths. These accounts say much more about the personal relationship of Christ to those who have encountered him today. Indeed, the Christ encounters that I have received rarely exhibit a focus other than that of the individual recipients and their close relationships at the time. In almost all of the cases, Christ seems to manifest himself to communicate above all else the simple fact of his love for the person during a difficult time in his or her life.

Consequently, while Christ encounters may provide little information that specifically addresses God's perspective on the collective concerns of mankind, they do reveal in detail and heartfelt depth the type of relationship one may apparently enjoy with Christ today.

". . . but I will see you again, and your hearts will rejoice,
and no one will take your joy from you."
John 16:22

8

Confirmation

"Wherever I am, I will always remember you."
M.L.P.

THE CHRIST ENCOUNTERS EXAMINED IN THIS
volume appear to be, most essentially, a profound expression of love
and acceptance. And yet each affects the witness according to the
need at the time. If a person is ill, the experience can exert a physically healing effect, or at least alleviate pain and suffering. If a
person is emotionally distraught, the Christ encounter can
eliminate fear, doubt, depression, and other destructive emotions. If
the person has avoided resolving an important obstacle to his or her
own growth, the Christ figure can confront the witness with this
unfinished business and also provide an opportunity to work
through the impasse. When the individual needs instruction or
guidance, the experience can point the way. In essence, the Christ

encounter typically illuminates and compensates for whatever is out of balance. After bringing problems to light, the Christ figure's influence offsets physical, emotional, or spiritual conditions which have gone awry and reestablishes a more healthy balance.

Some Christ encounters occur at times when people do not seem to need a corrective intervention. We have already examined one type that seems to come from "out of the blue"—the awakening Christ encounter. In these experiences, Christ seems "merely" to announce his presence as a way to awaken the person to what could become an ongoing relationship with him.

Another type—and the topic of this chapter—is represented by those accounts in which Christ bestows praise or confirmation upon the person. I have termed these accounts "confirmational" Christ encounters. Christ's intervention leaves the witnesses feeling reassured and blessed by his love. He seems to manifest principally to praise the person for work already done, or simply to express his approval for the person without direct reference to anything else.

Awakening and confirmational Christ encounters appear to differ from the other types. Many of the awakening and confirmational witnesses were not experiencing any apparent problems when their Christ encounters happened. At least, this is the impression created by their testimonies. Unless we embrace a rather shallow view of happiness, it is likely that few, if any, of us have fully "arrived," even during times of relative stability and contentment. It may be that the awakening and confirmation encounters address a need that always exists—to resolve the problem of our own perceived separateness from God.

The fact that such experiences occur at all is significant. They offset the possible impression that Christ encounters occur only during times of crisis. Generally speaking, the other types of accounts reveal a being who intervenes to point out, correct, or heal imbalances. In contrast, many of the awakening and confirmation accounts reveal a being who is active and imminent in a person's life during the good times as well as the bad.

The following Christ encounter took place as the witness—an artist—was experiencing a deep sense of meaning about her work. As she feels the positive emotions about her art, Christ appears to her, reinforcing her feelings and her own assessment of her work.

I was busy preparing for a two-person art show that my girl-friend and I had every year. It was April 1983. I always left everything until the last month. Our show opened in May, so every spare minute between working a full-time job was devoted to the show. I started out with two pastel drawings, very light, dreamy drawings called "Dream Roads" and "Transcending." My other pieces were sculpture. I never really planned what I was going to do. Ideas seemed to just come to me. . . .

I was working on a sculpture in my studio, and I was bent over in front of the north window sawing wood with a handsaw. I felt wonderful. Then I looked up to the hallway leading into the room. I saw the lower half of a person in leather sandals and the bottom of a white robe that was so white that it wasn't really solid . . . like bright burning white light. I did not see his face. I looked only from the waist down, and only for a few seconds. I knew it was Jesus. I continued my sawing. The message was loud and clear. I was doing what I was meant to do. I felt very happy. (R.N.)

R.N. experienced Christ's presence as a powerful confirmation of the path she had already taken in her work. But she went on to admit that while the sculptures made her immensely happy, they were never a commercial success. This suggests that Christ manifested as a confirmation of her state of mind and heart awakened by the chosen course of action. But he did not come to guarantee the worldly success of the project itself. To think otherwise might have left her feeling tricked.

Just as Christ seemed to manifest to R.N. to confirm her elevated mood and sense of direction, the following encounter took place as a young girl gradually entered a state of rapture as she sang her favorite hymn. Her emotional and spiritual openness seemed to establish a context in which she could then turn and see what is perhaps always there—Jesus walking beside her.

Ever since my sixteenth year, I've wanted to share an experience which occurred when I was a high-school sophomore. I have never shared it with anyone except my mother and best friend, lest someone think I was either lying or hallucinating.

On the maternal side of my family I have Cherokee ancestors; on the other, my grandparents and grandaunt were Shakers. Both Indians and Shakers believe that psychic gifts come from God, and that these gifts include visions and "Dreaming True."

With such a background, it was fairly easy to accept my psychic gifts—until the day I saw Jesus. Although I knew that it was a true and valid experience, I found it both exalting and unsettling.

I was walking the three miles to the point where I caught the school bus in Seddy, Tennessee. Although I can't carry a tune, I was caught up in a sense of at-oneness with God, and

*began singing "I Come to the Garden Alone" as I trudged
along.*

*As I came to the part of the song that says, "And he walks
with me and he talks with me, And he tells me I am his own,"
I sensed a presence walking beside me, on my right. I was in
a kind of altered state of consciousness in that moment; a
state of spiritual rapture. I have never since felt so exalted,
spiritually speaking. As I turned to look, I saw Christ in a
three-dimensional form with red-blond hair, blue eyes, and
robes of blue. At first I thought he was a "real" person
walking beside me.*

*I was not on any medication and have never halluci-
nated. The vision was totally impromptu, incited perhaps by
the rapture I felt as I sang, off-key, my favorite hymn. (M.H.)*

M.H. had other encounters in the ensuing years. In one
memorable "lucid dream"—one in which she was fully aware that
she was dreaming—she again met Christ face-to-face.

*Forty years later, I had a lucid dream of Christ which seems
as real as any event in my life. Today, I remember the dream
in as much detail and as vividly as I did upon awakening on
the night the dream occurred.*

*The dream began in black and white, but later turned
into vivid color.*

*It started with my being on the edge of a slippery, slimy
riverbank on a pitch-black night. I couldn't see where I was
going, so I crawled along on my hands and knees. Every now
and then I would slip over the edge of the bank, and down its
side, but I would catch onto a protruding branch or some
other projection, which I could not see. I seemed to know that*

if, in the darkness, I slid down the black, slimy bank into the equally black river, I would be lost forever.

Then ahead, I saw a white light. I crawled toward it, and came to a brightly lighted clearing. Now, everything was in brilliant color, and beautiful. At the edge of the forest grew vividly colored flowers. The grass was a bright emerald green.

In the center of the clearing stood a beautiful southern mansion which gleamed like alabaster. I walked up to the door, knocked, and then entered. I was now in a circular-shaped foyer with marble floors. To my right was a circular staircase which led to a mezzanine balcony.

On the balcony stood the Christ I had seen in my youth, again wearing a blue robe. He was smiling the same sweet, tender smile, and held his arms out to welcome me. I felt that I had come home at last.

Remembering the earlier vision and the more recent dream has helped me face three cancer surgeries and four chronic catastrophic illnesses. I will be in the hospital by the time you receive this for another operation for cancer. (M.H.)

M.H.'s lucid dream resembles the kind of perceptually vivid experiences reported by those who presumably gain a glimpse of the afterlife during a near-death experience. The vivid colors and emerald-colored grass are reminiscent of Betty Eadie's magnificent near-death experience described in *Embraced by the Light* (Goldleaf Press, 1992). Although M.H. was not in any kind of physical trauma during the dream, her struggle with chronic illnesses might have brought on this "preview" of her eventual destiny beyond death. Perhaps the earlier part of the dream—her efforts to avoid falling into the river—symbolized both her struggle to cling to life and her commitment to remain faithfully focused on her eventual destiny—to be with him again.

The following account also has the earmarks of a near-death experience. But the witness was not, as far as she knew, clinically dead—only recovering from an operation.

At the age of thirteen, as I was coming to following surgery, I found myself held in the arms of a being of white light. I remember feeling very safe and at peace. It felt as if I was a baby being cradled. I turned to look up toward the face and recognized it as Jesus. His robe was brilliant white and he had the warmest loving smile. No words were spoken but I did not want to leave.

As I felt myself being lowered to the bed (and the pain I knew I'd wake up to) I could see and feel his arms and hands placing me back in my body on the hospital bed. I could hear him say that it wasn't time for me to stay yet. I could feel his love and wanted to hang on to that feeling forever.

When I woke up and saw my mother, I was excited and asked her if she had seen him. I was looking toward where I had felt myself come from. I was hoping to still see him, I guess. No one in the ward had seen anything unusual. My parents always explained it as the drugs from surgery, but to this day I remember the spiritual sight and feel of the experience.

As I read and study, I accept the experience for exactly what it was: a Christ encounter on a plane other than the one on which we live. (S.G.)

S.G.'s experience was one of profound love, joy, and comfort. Her relationship with Christ was the only issue at hand. Not her beliefs, not her mission in life, not her good deeds, not her sins. Only his love for her. Understandably, this kind of consoling experience leaves many of us focused on Christ's role as comforter in our lives.

Even when a confirming experience of his love is imminent, it is not always easy to accept it. In the following account, a young woman experiences a simple yet powerfully direct confirmation from Jesus—but only after trying to avoid him.

In the dream I was in a classroom lined with benches around the walls, with blackboards at one end. Jesus was sleeping on a bench at the back of the classroom, and the feeling was one of anticipating his waking—like the fishermen had at sea— to calm the storm.

As he awakened, I walked toward the door. I was afraid he would look at me, and I felt too unworthy, so I hoped he would not. But he turned and looked at me and came toward me. He then gathered me up to hug me. His appearance then changed to the form of an old East Indian man, with graying hair cut very short, and a distant twinkle in his eyes. (R.A.)

R.A. reminds us that it is difficult to feel worthy of Christ's love. If he appeared in our midst today, many of us would probably actively avoid him, as she did, out of our sense of inadequacy. But he did not wait for R.A. to declare herself worthy: He sought her out. He did not permit her feelings to prevent an encounter. What a statement her experience makes about Christ's willingness to affirm us in spite of our own low self-esteem! The experience itself is a gift, a confirmation of God's love in spite of R.A.'s self-assessment.

In a vivid waking vision, another woman experiences a similar confirmation of her acceptability in Christ's eyes.

I was in Tulsa, Oklahoma, at a prayer meeting (1973 or 1974), in the living room of a teacher. There were three rows of people in the living room.

Jesus first appeared to me on the fireplace wall. He was very etheric looking, and I could see right through him. On one particular night, we asked for a blessing. I saw him look up and raise his left hand. Then, moving from left to right, he passed his hand over the group. As his hand passed, a tongue of flame appeared on top of everyone's head. The flame appeared in the crown area on the right side of the head. I even felt the flame. Then we started praying for people.

Jesus came down into the center of the group and became as solid and as clear as everyone else that was there. I even saw clearly how his sandals were laced.

He held out his arms to welcome everyone. The look on his face was like a mother looking at her newborn child.

The blue of his eyes was like nothing I've ever seen. It was like the whole eye was blue. A blue that was bluer than the sky.

I asked him, "Why me? I'm not worthy to be shown you. There are others in this group more worthy than me."

He said, "Why not you?"

I ended the prayer meeting with tears running down my face. (V.H.)

This dramatic account indicates that no matter how vivid Christ may appear to a person, others may still be unable to perceive his presence. V.H.'s own sense of unimportance tells her that she did not earn the experience. Her puzzled questioning reflects this realization. Significantly, Christ does not say, "But you did deserve it." That would have made his manifestation to V.H. a form of reward. Given what he said, one can conclude that V.H.'s "goodness" or "sinfulness" was not the issue at all. Christ's love is the issue, and the experience simply confirmed it. His elegant and powerful question essentially challenges her—or anyone for that matter—to present anything about herself that could possibly over-shadow his love of her. The question "Why not you?" is, perhaps, a succinct statement of his radically inclusive spirit, of his accept-ance of each and every person he meets.

Christians have often invoked Christ's presence through ritually enacting significant moments in Jesus' life. From the practice of Holy Communion to the pope's annual retracing of Jesus' final walk, Christians have historically turned to ritual reen-actment as a way of increasing their sense of Christ's abiding presence in their lives. Many have traveled to the Holy Land and walked the dusty roads that Jesus and his disciples walked two thousand years ago.

In the following account, a woman sees Jesus walking toward her on the banks of the River Jordan.

A very special moment with the Master came in 1975 while visiting in the Holy Land.

My husband had a dear Jewish friend who lived in Tel Aviv. He arranged for our lodging and planned tours for us when he and his wife were not free to be with us.

On a tour that took us to the Jordan River, I managed to linger behind the tour group. I sat, or stood—I cannot remember now—by the riverbank. My thoughts were of Jesus and his baptism by John.

Suddenly, I looked up to see the figure of Jesus walking toward me. Today, I cannot remember what I did or said (or if I spoke). He did not speak, but it was more than a "picturing of him." Quietly, he faded from my vision. I was filled with a renewal of Spirit. (M.E.)

Once again, so much was conveyed and confirmed in a few silent moments of encountering Christ: his availability, his aliveness, and his love for M.E. About the seeming brevity of such experiences, Saint Teresa of Avila once said that "in an instant the mind learns so many things at once that if the imagination and the intellect spend years striving to enumerate them, they could not recall a thousandth part of them."[29]

If we take Saint Teresa's words to heart, then brevity is no measure of the significance of a Christ encounter.

Perhaps the ultimate confirmation is to be ushered by him into the realization that we are, as he is, boundless spiritual beings. The following account was submitted by a thirty-six-year-old woman who, at the time of the experience, was a member of a religious order. Like many of the witnesses of the other Christ encounters, she has had several encounters with Christ.

I was meditating in the chapel with the other members of the order. Our collective prayers were to Jesus, in a spirit of giving ourselves to him as channels of blessing and service.

Then I felt the loving presence with me and saw white light pouring into my body and radiating from my face. As I meditated upon this light and Jesus, I was led through an experience like a near-death experience. I passed through a tunnel-like passage, into an area of soft blue light; deeper into a dark area; and finally into the midst of a brilliant, shining sun. I remained there in this light like no other and heard his voice different and separate from the still, small voice of my intuition. He said only, "Lo, I am with you always, even unto the end."

I was shown and told a lot from a perspective of a higher knowing but don't remember what was given. What has remained with me is that I experienced myself as a perfect, whole being with no sense of boundaries or limitations. I was in a complete union and peace with God: There was no separation, not even a concept of being separate. Creator and creation were one in a vibration of infinite love. I was overwhelmed by the beauty and love that I experienced for myself and all other people as at that moment.

In coming out of the meditation, I remember feeling a sense of grief or loss at not being able to maintain the level of conscious awareness and manifestation of that true self in my everyday life. It was like feeling the atmosphere change when you come down from the high altitudes of a mountain. I wondered why I could not just be that greater "me" all the time. My personality felt like a burden I was carrying around. But I knew that this was the challenge and purpose of my life now—to manifest that awareness and to see others in that light. (C.N.)

C.N.'s experience of loss as she returned to her "ordinary" state of consciousness underscores one of the dilemmas posed by the Christ encounter: The witness is thereafter consigned to live with the memory of what may never again occur.

The confirmational Christ encounter can resemble a parent-child encounter, in which the parent—beyond requiring anything of the child—simply overflows with love and praise toward the child. This next recipient experienced silent but profound confirmation as she saw Jesus briefly manifest to her while she was driving.

The first time Jesus appeared to me was when I was driving my car through Cranston, a city near Rhode Island's capital. He appeared only briefly. . . . He was sitting in the passenger seat with the seat belt on! He looked at me, but said nothing. The love and peace I felt from him were overpowering. He was looking at me, not with pride, but with pleasure. In other words, he seemed pleased with me and looked at me with the type of love a father would have for his child. (M.W.)

Even though M.W. experienced only love and confirmation from Jesus, she was still left wondering, *Why me, and what next?* When she told her minister about the encounter, she found him supporting the idea that God was calling her. But to do what? While she admits that she gets scared because she doesn't feel worthy of this attention, she says that she's "more afraid of not doing what God wants me to do." She goes on to say, "It's no exaggeration to say that I am going through probably the most humbling and exhilarating period of my life. I understand now why the apostles just stopped what they were doing and followed Christ. If he appears to me again and tells me to do whatever, I will do it."

It is understandable that M.W. assumed that Christ has some specific agenda for her. But this assumption runs the risk of over-looking the most obvious implication of her encounter—that he manifested to express his pleasure. There is no evidence that he intended to inaugurate a new course of action. As already suggested, the Christ encounter stimulates a search for greater meaning and new directions. Whether it is his intent that we should be so galvanized as to pursue a dramatic new course in life is by no means clear from many of the confirmational type of encounters.

Through the following encounter, a fifty-two-year-old RN came to realize that Christ is "alive now in the present." P.B.'s experience is a remarkably luminous and cosmic example of a confirmational Christ encounter. In addition to portraying Christ as a light being with a sublimely beautiful human side, it includes, as well, the presence of angelic or spirit "guides" who serve as intermediaries between her and the Christ being.

I dream that I am with my spiritual guides. They are teaching me and giving me a progress report. One smiles at me and says he is pleased with my progress, that I am "becoming." He has never smiled at me before and this is very gratifying to me. They both say that I am now ready to meet someone.

We fly together through clouds. It is beautiful. Straight ahead, the clouds appear as if the sun is shining behind them, trying to break through.

I can see now that behind the clouds is a very bright, white-blue light, sort of like the sun, but not exactly. There are blue-white, white-blue, shimmering crystalline light rays streaming above, below, and through the clouds. It is just indescribably beautiful.

The clouds begin to part and the light shines through. It is extremely bright, but does not hurt my eyes. I feel myself being drawn toward the light. It emits something so soothing, so comfortable, so assuring. I am filled inside and out with all these feelings of love, joy, peacefulness, and utmost content.

Moving on toward the light, I see that it is a being—it is alive, vibrantly alive! Without a doubt, this is the most alive being I have ever encountered. He is an absolutely radiantly beautiful, incredible being, standing in the midst of the most beautiful, spectacular, shimmering, shining, glowing light which he is emitting. He is the light; the light is him. As he moves, the light rays radiate his movements. There are no words. No words exist to describe his beauty and person. Sublime, he is truly sublime.

I am close enough now to see his face. I recognize him. It is Jesus, the Christ. His eyes! Such compassion! He is looking at me. He knows me inside and out! and it's okay. I feel such compassion, acceptance, warmth, kindness, and understanding coming from him. There is a radiation of these feelings from him.

He shows me the earth, hanging in space. There is something like a halo of shimmering blue, pink, glowing light coming from it. I realize that it is the earth's aura. The earth is a living being, too. Looking at it from here, I think, "No wonder I chose to come here."

The earth is wonderful, beautiful, and inviting. It beckons to me. I feel such a part of it.

Then he shows me something like a motion picture of the evolution of the earth. I see that the earth is progressing, moving, and responding to a universal law.

There is a new stage of evolution, beginning now. The earth is entering a stage of attunement, an at-one-ment. And I understand at once why I am here at this time and why I feel what I feel.

So that was my dream. On awakening, I was so overwhelmed with feelings that I cried. I knew it was more than an ordinary dream, but I didn't know exactly what it was. I still don't.

Somehow, in the sleep state, I entered into another dimension of reality; one that was much more real than this one. Christ is alive; he is a living Christ, existing in the present. He is truly present among us and exists with each of us in the "now." Since this dream, I have had a real sense of his presence within me. There still exists that soothing, comfortable, peaceful, presence within me like I felt in the dream. It is not as intense, but it is definitely still there, and at all times. I feel it inside of me the most when I am sad or depressed.

I have an understanding now that my personal wants are not as important. They have taken a lower priority. The most important thing is what he wants for me. So this is my prayer each and every day, that his will be done through me. And some truly amazing things have happened. It is as if I am being guided by unseen hands in the directions I need to grow spiritually.

I am an ordinary person. I don't know why I had such a special experience. I feel so humbled and unworthy somehow. Yet the message rings true and clear. I am here for a reason, a purpose. And I must do my part. (P.B.)

P.B.'s confirming, life-transforming experience anchors her sense of life purpose. The connection comes from a feeling of partnership with Christ. But a relationship with him can sometimes be a bond that develops over time. Surely this was true for a sixty-year-old woman who had dedicated her life to searching for spiritual truth from the early age of eight.

I laid down the ideal of my life at age eight: Seek ye first the kingdom of God. For many years I have searched and studied the great teachers. So when at age sixty I had this vision, I understood it as the culmination of all my previous years of effort.

While meditating, I suddenly became aware of a magnificent steady sound! It was a high-frequency note that reminded me of Beethoven's "Sounds of the Spheres" and Bach's eternal motion melody.

I looked up and saw the Lord. He was a brilliant white figure flying from left to right. His arms stretched wide so his garments were his wings. His motion forward made that beautiful sound! On the white garment, every inch was covered with human faces. First I was shocked, but I quickly understood its symbolic meaning: The whole universe, mankind included, was the body of Christ!

Later, I encountered him again. As I sat, a beautiful, all-silver, androgynous figure appeared. I knew that he was the Lord. Without moving, he said; "I love you till the end of times."

This sentence has become my refuge, my source and my guide. Such a meeting after sixty years!

I have kept this encounter to myself for many years. You are the second person I share it with. (3rd C.M.)

C.M. received the ultimate blessing—a gift of timeless love from the one who is the source of all her strength and the end of all her searching. It would be wonderful if each of us could know, as she did, that this was his gift to us. It's one thing to accept it on faith, and another thing to hear it, to know it.

Christ bestows this ultimate timeless gift upon another in the following Christ encounters. The witness is M.L.P., a woman whose other accounts appear in earlier chapters. Here she points out that her earlier experiences were characterized by Christ appearing to her as all-powerful master and healer. In the accounts that follow, however, the relationship changes to a more balanced, reciprocal exchange of love and common goals. As the final Christ encounters presented in this book, they reveal a possibility that few of the other accounts directly allude to—that the Christ encounter provides an opportunity to love him as he loves us.

In the dream, I knew that I was on my way to my appointment with him. I was a child, about nine years old, and I was glad that I had this special meeting with him.

The meeting was on the second floor. The stairs were on the outside of the building. I opened the door, walked a few steps down a hallway, and turned into the room on my right.

He was the only light in the room. It was bare. No other furniture than the straight chair he sat on in the center of the room. He was wearing a white robe.

His smile was warm and welcoming and my heart rushed to him and urged me to follow. I loved him so much. But then I realized that this was something I could give him; that is, if I didn't take up this time with him, it would give him a few minutes to himself.

He sensed this immediately and was grateful for my gift, knowing what a sacrifice it was to leave him.

He smiled, a smile filled with gratefulness.

"As long as I live," he started to say, and then stopped, knowing that I would misunderstand. He began again: "Wherever I am, I will always remember you."

I backed out of the room, and when I reached the hall I heard soldiers coming up the stairs.

"They're going to crucify him!" I heard my mind scream and I ran screaming down the hall, down the stairs past the soldiers and into consciousness.

This dream was about two years after my first experience. (M.L.P.)

Of course, there is no way to determine whether this event ever happened before: That's really not important. But what M.L.P. experienced—and, even more importantly, what she *did* in this encounter—had a profound impact on her life thereafter. The words Jesus spoke to her show us again that his commitment to those who love him transcends time and death, and can sustain us in the absence of external reassurances. M.L.P.'s experience also reveals an astounding possibility: that what we do, and how we love, somehow sustains him in return.

M.L.P.'s next two experiences, which took place several years later, also reveal the sense of an evolving partnership.

It was during a time when I was meditating at 2:00 in the morning. However, this experience was in the evening. I was alone in my living room. The evening had a strange quality about it . . . a sense of hushed expectancy. Not spooky, but more expectant. Charged, but in a gentle electricity, not the riveting kind. I was standing, doing nothing, when I heard him say: "And in a little while, I'll be with you." Nothing more was said, nothing more was needed. (M.L.P.)

The last time I saw Jesus was a face-to-face encounter. I remember only this: I was looking him straight in the eye, person to person. I heard a strength in my voice as I said, almost demanding, not so much asking as requiring: "If I do this, will you be there?"

That was several years ago. I don't know what I agreed to do, but I know that he pledged to be there. (M.L.P.)

As we review M.L.P.'s Christ encounters, we find that Christ first comes to her bedside and kneels to pray with her (Chapter 2), thus awakening her to the possibility of an ongoing relationship with him. Soon after, a being of pure light heals her physical pain and takes her out of her body to be with him (Chapter 3). Then years later, she bestows the same "Christlike" love upon him that he has given to her. And finally, her last two accounts point to the pursuit of mutual goals and an eventual reunion with him.

M.L.P.'s experience suggests that our relationship with Christ can evolve over time—from an initial act of commitment, which may or may not coincide with an actual encounter, to a full partnership with him. This evolving relationship shows our own destiny to be one with him in spirit. It presents, at once, an exalted view of our importance in the larger scheme of things, as well as a humbling vision of the awesome responsibilities that stand between us and the greater destiny that awaits us.

> *"And remember, I am with you always,*
> *to the end of the age."*
> Matthew 28:20

9

A Cloud of Witnesses

"Now is the time for me to lay down my cross,
and for you to carry it."
G.S.S.

IT IS ENCOURAGING THAT SO MANY INDIVIDUALS have had experiences that point to Christ's continuing presence in their lives. Knowing this may give others greater hope that they will eventually enjoy direct encounters with him. But there is an equally profound possibility that I invite you to consider at this point—*you have already experienced Christ's presence through your empathic response to the experiences of others.*

I saw evidence of this while I was leading a therapeutic group some time ago. As I was leading my Friday night therapy group, a man told of a Christ encounter that ushered him out of alcoholism into a life of sobriety. He had been a member of the group for six months, but had never mentioned the experience that had become the turning point of his life.

He was alone in his apartment, and he came to the stark realization that alcohol had controlled his life since he was twelve. He said to himself, "No more." He wandered about the apartment considering all that would have to change in his life. He stopped to look out of a window, and saw a shimmering image. Then the clear image of Jesus appeared. As he stared spellbound at the image, he found himself in the backyard of his childhood home, imprisoned in a cage. It was the home where he grew up with a domineering father and an alcoholic mother. As a child, he had been caught between them, seeking futilely to please his judgmental father, and trying desperately to heal his mother with his love.

Suddenly, in his vision, the bars of the cage lifted, and he was free. This experience became the first step in his difficult journey toward recovery, and has since served as a beacon during times of confusion and despair.

The group was transfixed by the man's tearful story. One woman in particular, an atheist, was moved to speak. She first acknowledged that she had never had such an encounter. But then she stated that she now had a clear sense of what it would be like to have something so important and so central in her life—an event to which everything would have to answer. She said she finally realized what people meant when they speak of having an ideal. She has since awakened to her own spirituality, and has recently joined the Episcopal church.

The man's story seemed to have a quickening effect on all of us. I, for one, felt drawn into Christ's presence through his experience. This event demonstrated to me once again that *a Christ encounter gathers new witnesses through its sharing.*

Having read this book, you have indirectly experienced dozens of Christ encounters. And you have probably been deeply touched by some of them in particular. Like the woman in my Friday night group, we become witnesses to Christ's manifestation through our response to these sacred encounters.

This idea may seem strange, especially if you haven't had a direct Christ encounter of your own. You may wonder how your experience of reading these accounts can be compared to meeting Christ face-to-face.

Think of it this way. Only a few people actually met Jesus during his brief ministry. And of those who did, still fewer understood him enough to be responsive to his teachings. Isn't it probably true that his disciples and other true followers—both then and now—are simply those who respond to him with love and commitment? Doesn't it also make sense that he realized that these same followers would tell others about their experiences, thereby expanding his reach into the hearts of men and women everywhere? Indeed, his presence was, and still is, a powerful expanding influence that—like the fishes and loaves—multiplies upon contact with others.

What does it matter whether this response comes through our own direct encounters or through the experiences of others? When we let go of the need to see him, we may find that we already *know* him through the testimonies of others.

Thus we come together as witnesses. We meet on a common ground through our common response to the Spirit impelling these experiences.

A Call to Discipleship?

What do these experiences mean to *us*? What are *we* called to do? These are difficult questions. But the evidence provided by the Christ encounters strongly suggests one answer: Christ manifests to call us into a closer relationship with him. And he seems to expect us to strive to remain in constant relationship, or communion, with him.

But what kind of ongoing relationship does he want? These accounts coincide with the scriptural record in revealing a Master who, in spite of the imperfections in those he chooses, lifts them into partnership with him. It's the same spirit of partnership that called common fishermen to become fishers of men. It's the same spirit that summoned Paul to become apostle to the Gentiles. It's the same spirit that could overlook the betraying nature of Peter and see in him a secure foundation for his church. It's a spirit that calls us to be no less than disciples, even though we remain seriously afflicted by weaknesses and imperfections.

Even if we could bring ourselves to accept the full measure of this invitation, we might still be left wondering what discipleship means *in our everyday lives*. I can only answer this for myself. To me, it simply means living in such close relationship with him that my thoughts and actions are considered against the question, What would *he* do? In other words, it means imitating him to the best of my ability so I can eventually become as he is.

While this might sound presumptuous, I believe it's all that Christ calls us to do. In support of this, C.S. Lewis says that the imitation of Christ "is not one among many jobs a Christian has to do; and it is not a sort of special exercise for the top class. It is the whole of Christianity. Christianity offers nothing else at all."[30]

Potential Pitfalls

Of course, most of us will doubtless slip and fall many times as we attempt to imitate him and become full partners with him. What are the likely pitfalls? I can think of three obvious ones.

Imposing our own narrow desires. We become so confident we are serving him that we can inadvertently cease listening for his promptings. We begin to take matters into our own hands. Judas exemplifies one who did this by trying to force Jesus to reveal himself. Apparently, he thought that if he backed Jesus into a corner, he would come out in a blaze of power and glory. He was wrong and saw the disastrous consequences of his arrogance. To those of us who are willing to accept a closer relationship with him, we must resist the tendency to require Christ to come forth according to our narrow desires and wishes.

A dream effectively underscored this flaw in me.

> *I was back in the time of Jesus, among his close followers. We had been staying in the countryside for some time and did not understand why Jesus was hesitating to go into Jerusalem. We all believed that his entrance into Jerusalem would be the momentous event we had awaited for some time. People would finally proclaim him for who he was. We were all very impatient to be going.*
>
> *Finally, Jesus told us that it was time to go. As I left the building where we had been staying, I looked up and saw Jesus looking at me out of an upstairs window. His face showed love but deep sadness. I waved enthusiastically. He smiled at me without saying anything, like a parent who accepts that his child doesn't understand. Then we all took off hurriedly in the direction of Jerusalem. As I awoke, I realized in shock what I had failed to grasp in the dream— that he was going to his death.* (G.S.S.)

Waiting on his promptings can be difficult as long as we cling to what we believe is important. Whenever we try to impose our priorities without regard to his, we run the risk of crucifying the very Spirit we claim to serve. It is a problem that no doubt afflicts many of us from time to time.

My friend Mark discovered this sobering tendency in himself. He had just finished a demanding four-day conference in which he had been one of the guest speakers. He lay down to take a nap, feeling like he had really been working diligently and effectively for God during the previous days. As he drifted off to sleep, a dream unfolded before he lost consciousness. His full wakefulness carried over into the "lucid" dream without a break.

He found himself with three other men and immediately recalled that he met with them every day in his dreams. They formed a group who had a teacher.

As their teacher joined them, Mark saw it was Christ himself. Christ began his daily instruction, but Mark's thoughts were already jumping ahead to what he knew would be the culmination of the daily lesson. He remembered that at the end of each lesson, Christ always gave them a "word for the day." This word expressed the essence of what each of them would be challenged to learn during the upcoming day.

Mark felt an extraordinary desire to know that word. It was as if he had had nothing to drink for a whole day, and the upcoming word was like a glass of water. He was sure his companions felt the same way. Consequently, he was not paying careful attention to what Christ was saying. Instead, Mark was trying to figure out what the word would probably be—as if the new word would logically follow the words they had been assigned before.

Suddenly, he realized that Christ was coming to that part of the lesson where the word would be given. But to his shock and embarrassment, Christ said, "I'm unable to give the word today because one among you is impatient and unable to let go and trust." He named no one, but Mark knew it was obviously him. Upon awakening, he realized that Christ had—lovingly and firmly—held up a magnifying glass to his tendency to preempt the Spirit with his own agenda.

Clinging to Experiences. Another problem that confronts us as modern disciples is the tendency to become more attached to the experience of his presence than to the spiritual life to which he calls us. This is especially likely for those who have already experienced him in a direct way. And it gives a contemporary meaning to Jesus' words to Thomas, "Blessed are those who have not seen and yet have come to believe." (John 20:29).

Longfellow's poem, "A Theologian's Tale: The Legend Beautiful," eloquently describes the problem of becoming attached to spiritual experiences. Further, Longfellow makes an even stronger statement—that Christ's continuing presence in our lives *depends* on our putting service to others above our enjoyment of his presence.

The poem opens with a monk praying in his cell. Suddenly, a radiant vision of Christ appears before him. He is overwhelmed with love and ecstasy, and is loathe to leave his cell to go about his daily duties. Specifically, the poor await him and his brothers for the food they provide them each day. The monk finally tears himself away, and finds that the day unfolds magically. Each ordinary duty takes on an air of supreme meaning, and the poor people seem particularly blessed by the food provided by the monks. When he hurries back to his cell at the end of the day, hoping that that vision is still there for him, he finds that Jesus has waited for him. Later, when Jesus finally departs, the monk hears him say: "If thou hadst stayed, I must have fled."

It is ironic that the experience of his presence can come to be an obstacle to our serving him. But anyone who has experienced a Christ encounter can easily become attached to the awesome gift of his confirming presence. Then, rather than forging ahead on our own, we feel inadequate if we can't recapture that sense of presence. My own experience again serves as a good example.

For several years in my early to mid-twenties, I enjoyed numerous deep spiritual experiences and Christ encounters. But then, as the years passed, the experiences slowly diminished in frequency. I missed them, and I wondered if I was doing something wrong. Then I had a revealing dream which helped me to see the purpose operating behind the decrease in my experiences with him.

I was again with his followers and friends. It seemed that we all knew that soon he would no longer be with us. We were saying good-bye to him, one by one. I approached him and embraced him, sobbing deeply. As I turned to walk away, I saw a man whom I knew to be Peter. We embraced each other, sharing our sense of imminent loss. I was profoundly saddened, but I was also aware that Jesus had told us that his departure was necessary for us to develop more fully on our own. (G.S.S.)

No matter how much we claim to be our own persons, the mere presence of our parents—and other persons of authority—can perpetuate our dependency on them. Eventually, we must strike out on our own before we can mature fully. Similarly, the experience of Christ's abiding presence can, at times, overshadow our own abilities to become spiritually involved in the lives of those around us.

Fear of Surrendering. Finally, I believe there is a third significant impediment to our accepting the mantle of discipleship: our fear of surrendering fully to a relationship with him. We think we can keep something back for ourselves. We want to strike a bargain in which he gets what he wants and we get what we want. C.S. Lewis compares this attitude to that of an honest man paying his taxes. "He pays them all right, but he does hope that there be enough left over for him to live on." This does not seem to be what Christ has in mind. The Christian way, Lewis contends, is much harder and much easier. "Christ says, 'Give me all.' " [31]

Something in us doesn't like this idea. We tremble at the thought of turning over our lives.

Not long ago, as I awoke one morning, I had an experience which is quite rare for me to have. I heard a voice, and it clearly said to me, "Now is the time for me to lay down my cross, and for you to carry it." In reflection, I believe that the cross signifies to me the exquisite burden of surrendering completely to a life of serving the Master.

Further, I believe that my whole life—and perhaps yours, too—comes down to a single question: *Will you?*

Christ can awaken us to a relationship with him. As the great physician, he can heal our bodies and our hearts, and console us during times of necessary losses. As taskmaster, he can confront and initiate us, encouraging us to remove obstacles to a closer relationship with him. As the consummate teacher, he can instruct and guide us into areas of new growth. And as the bridegroom, he can come to reassure us that we are, above all else, loved.

Out of this process can come the realization that *he is alive*, that we are called by a living Master to do more than we've ever imagined. To become his partners and to accept the mantle of discipleship. To imitate him and to grow into a likeness of him.

Short of our full arrival, it might mean falling into error. It might mean imposing our own selfish agendas for a season. It might mean walking alone for long periods without the experience of his consoling presence. Finally, it might mean facing our fears of surrendering fully to a relationship with him.

Therefore, since we are surrounded by so great a cloud of witnesses, let us lay aside every weight and the sin that clings so closely, and let us run with perseverance the race that is set before us, looking to Jesus the pioneer and perfecter of our faith.

Hebrews 12:1–2a

Footnotes

[1] In *The Other Side of Silence* (Mahwah, N.J.: Paulist Press, 1976), *Companions on the Inner Way* (New York: Crossroads, 1983), and *Reaching: The Journey to Fulfillment* (San Francisco: Harper Collins, 1989), I described a variety of religious experiences. I have also laid out a view of reality that integrates this "other world" and "this world" and gives suggestions for those who wish to be closer to the religious dimensions of reality. I have described the importance of the dream-vision throughout Christian history in my book *God, Dreams and Revelation* (Minneapolis: Augsburg Fortress, 1992).

[2] *The Hymnal of the Protestant Episcopal Church in the United States of America.* (New York: The Church Pension Fund, 1943).

[3] Gordon, A. J. *How Christ Came to Church: A Spiritual Biography.* (New York: Revell, 1895).

[4] Nouwen, H. *Beyond the Mirror.* (New York: Crossroad, 1990).

[5] Greeley, A. M. *The Sociology of the Paranormal: A Reconnaissance.* (Beverly Hills: Sage, 1975).

[6] I have described many of my meditative encounters with Christ in the last chapter of *The Other Side of Silence.* I have described this particular experience in *Christo-Psychology* (New York: Crossroad, 1982).

[7] A lucid dream is a dream in which the dreamer is aware that he is dreaming. Lucid dreams have often been compared with, and considered equivalent to, out-of-body experiences, and are also associated with profound spiritual experiences.

8   Morton, T.R. *Knowing Jesus.* (Philadelphia: Westminster, 1974).

9   Chadwick, H. *The Early Church.* (New York: Dorset, 1986).

10 Daily, S. *Love Can Open Prison Doors.* (San Gabriel: Willing, 1938).

11 Supplement to reading 281–313 of the Edgar Cayce readings.

12 Ritchie, G. C., with Sherrill, E. *Return from Tomorrow.* (Waco: Chosen, 1978).

13 Moody, R. *Life After Life.* (St. Simons Island, Ga.: Mockingbird, 1975).

14 Ritchie, G.C. with Sherrill, E. Op. cit.

15 Fulop-Miller, R. *The Saints that Moved the World.* (New York: Thomas Crowell, 1945).

16 Griffin, W. *Clive Staples Lewis: A Dramatic Life.* (San Francisco: Harper and Row, 1986).

17 Jung, C.G. Psychological commentary on R. Wilhelm, *The Secret of the Golden Flower: A Chinese Book of Life.* (San Diego: Harcourt Brace Jovanovich, 1961).

18 Williams, C. *He Came Down From Heaven; and the Forgiveness of Sins.* (London: Faber and Faber, 1950).

19 Carpenter, H. *The Inklings.* (London: George Allen and Unwin, 1978).

20 Underhill, E. *Mysticism.* (New York: NAL, 1974).

21 Johnson, R. *The Fisher King and the Handless Maiden.* (New York: Harper Collins, 1993).

22 Brinkley, D. *Is There Life After Death?* Vol. II. (Dallas: The Eclectic Viewpoint, 1993).

23 Moore, T. *Care of the Soul.* (New York: Walker, 1992).

24 Lewis, C. S. *Letters to Malcolm: Chiefly on Prayer.* (New York: Harcourt Brace Jovanovich, 1964).

25 Kelsey, M. *Resurrection: Release from Oppression.* (Mahwah: Paulist, 1985).

26 Eadie, B.J. and C. Taylor. *Embraced by the Light.* (Placerville, CA: Gold Leaf Press, 1992).

[27] Teresa, Saint. *The Interior Castle.* (Garden City: Doubleday, 1961).

[28] Lewis, C. S. *Mere Christianity.* (New York: Macmillan, 1972, ca. 1943).

[29] Lewis, C.S. Ibid.

G. Scott Sparrow, Ed. D., is a spiritual mentor, psychotherapist, and writer who has published two books on Jesus and Mary. He received his bachelor's degree in psychology from the University of Texas at Austin, his master's degree in psychology from West Georgia College, and his doctorate in counseling from the College of William and Mary. His master's thesis and doctoral dissertation both focused on the phenomenon of "lucid dreaming," the experience of becoming aware that one is dreaming during the dream.

Dr. Sparrow has maintained a private practice in professional counseling for twenty years. He has lectured and taught courses across the United States on such topics as meditation, mystical experiences, and advanced dream work methods. He and his wife Kathy have three children and live in Arroyo City, Texas, where together they own the Kingfisher Inn and Guide Service, the only year-round fly fishing lodge on the Texas coast. They treasure the closeness to nature that their lifestyle affords them and consider it a spiritual calling to help people come into harmony with themselves in this remote, natural setting. Scott is a FFF-certified fly casting instructor and guides clients in the waters of the lower Laguna Madre.

CPSIA information can be obtained
at www.ICGtesting.com
Printed in the USA
BVHW050301020921
615811BV00007B/889